"In *You Be You*, Jamie inspires us to be all God created us to be, and do all we've been purposed to do. In her down to earth, tell it like it is, transparent, and humorous way, Jamie dispels the lies many of us believe about ourselves and invites us to accept that who we are in Christ is exactly who we need to be in order to outwork his purposes in the world. I love this woman, and you will love this book."

Christine Caine, founder A21 and Propel Women

"Fresh. Encouraging. Inspiring. In *You Be You*, Jamie Ivey invites readers to readily raise their voice, accept their God-given uniqueness, and find freedom in who they're becoming regardless of what they're doing. No matter what stage of life you're in, I'm confident this resource will make embracing your God-given identity and the eternal weight of your calling a palpable reality."

Louie Giglio, pastor of Passion City Church, founder of Passion Conferences, and author of *Not Forsaken*

"This book is an unhurried afternoon coffee date with a truth-telling friend who wants you to flourish. Jamie's honesty is refreshing and will point you to the God who has purpose for both your days and the giftings you possess."

Ruth Chou Simons, artist, national speaker, and bestselling author of *GraceLaced* and *Beholding and Becoming*; founder of GraceLaced.com

"Over the years, I've felt the sting of not measuring up. I've looked at others, wishing I had their spark, their ability, and their creativity. Looking around only made me less excited about what God put inside of me. I love that we have a good friend like Jamie who helps us recognize how our unique God-given talents were never meant to be buried under mounds of comparison. Instead they are to be recognized, celebrated, and used to bring God glory in the ways only we can. What a gift this book will be to your soul!"

Lysa TerKeurst, #1 *New York Times* bestselling author and president of Proverbs 31 Ministries

"In *You Be You*, Jamie Ivey helps you discover yourself while echoing the biblical truth necessary in order to do so. She takes you through a three step process of finding, accepting, and becoming yourself. I would recommend this book for anyone who has lost touch with or never really discovered their true self."

Alena Pitts, actress in *War Room* and
author of the *Lena in the Spotlight* series

"An empowering, game-changing book on purpose, calling, and the unrivaled value of your unique story. Jamie is an emphatic cheerleader for women in all seasons of life all over the world. Through her raw and vulnerable story-telling, hilarious perspective, and refreshingly practical application of biblical truths, you'll finish this book with the realization that living boldly in your calling—exactly as God made you—is more accessible than you've ever imagined. Give this book to every woman you know, and let's witness callings activated all over the world."

Hosanna Wong, author, spoken word artist,
and international speaker

"This book is so needed right now. In a world where we are desperately searching for direction and affirmation in all the wrong places, Jamie points us to the only One that matters. It's refreshingly honest and hopeful, and you'll find your shoulders relax as you read the truth in these pages. If you've ever felt like you lost yourself in life, read this book!"

Christy Wright, #1 national bestselling
author and host of *The Christy Wright Show*

"The vulnerable way that Jamie invites us to journey with her to the realizations she's arrived at is both refreshing and intimately inspiring. I am so very grateful for her gentle voice that speaks truth to places where it's sometimes hard to hear, only to bring healing to any person willing to listen. Her words shine a light with humor and sincerity, and to anybody willing, can genuinely help You Be You."

Laurie Crouch, host of *Better Together*,
Trinity Broadcasting Network

YOU
BE
YOU

Jamie Ivey

YOU BE YOU

why satisfaction
and success are
closer than you think

B&H
PUBLISHING
NASHVILLE, TENNESSEE

978-1-4627-4974-4

Published by B&H Publishing Group
Nashville, Tennessee

Dewey Decimal Classification: 248.84
Subject Heading: CHRISTIAN LIFE / SELF-ACCEPTANCE /
SELF-PERCEPTION

Cover photo by Dylan Reyes. Makeup by Lisa Proctor.
Styling by Amber Lehman and Beth Lehman, Jandyworks.

Published in association with Jenni Burke of Illuminate Literary
Agency: www.illuminateliterary.com

1 2 3 4 5 6 7 • 24 23 22 21 20

CONTENTS

Chapter 1

Good Time for a You-Turn?

I often wonder what it feels like to have a midlife crisis. Do you all of a sudden wake up one day and wonder if you're on the right track? Do you look around at your life and decide you're just not enjoying it anymore?

The times I've seen a midlife crisis played out on TV, it always involves a man leaving his wife and kids and driving off into the sunset in a sports car with a girl half his age. The happy couple is usually smiling real big, their hair blowing in the wind, and they most definitely have their hands up in the air.

Personally, I think that sounds like the *start* of a crisis, not the end of one.

So maybe a midlife crisis is not what I'm having. But I did sit in my counselor's office recently and ask her the kinds of questions that sound like a crisis of *some* sort could possibly be on my horizon.

- Who am I?
- What am I here for?
- Does this all matter?
- Who cares?
- Am I succeeding?
- Am I a failure?

The ironic thing about these questions is that it's not the first time I've asked them, and I doubt it will be the last. Maybe you've asked them too. It's our nature to want to matter, to be special, to make a difference, to win at life. And it's natural in our pursuit of these things to evaluate how we might be doing on that quest. It drives some of us into a counselor's office, some of us into late-night strategizing sessions with our girlfriends. Unfortunately it might even drive a few of us into that sports car analogy where we just plain choose a new life.

Sometimes for me, these questions become my way of trying to forecast the future, imagining what my life will be like when I'm old and gray. I can see my husband, Aaron, and myself sitting on our back porch watching our great-grandchildren frolicking in the pool. Because, yes, I'm almost certain we should live in a house with a pool so our kids will bring their kids, and their kids will bring *their* kids, and everyone will love going to the old person's house who has the great pool!

I see Aaron wobbling over to his grill where he's preparing burgers and veggies. I see myself pouring lemonade and bringing out the cookies. Store-bought, naturally. Because if I'm not baking homemade cookies at forty, you can be sure I won't be doing it at eighty. I might be old, but I won't be dumb! I'll still know how to get my people home to hang out with me.

A pool and good food. That ought to do it.

But seriously, I think looking ahead can be a healthy exercise, as long as the goal is to let it impact our *now*, our *today*. I once heard someone say (wisely, I thought), "Imagine who you want to be at eighty, then work backward to where you are now, and you'll see what you need to do to become the eighty-year-old you envision." Because death is coming for all of us. I know that sounds like the most morbid way of all to open a book, but it's where I think we should start. *At the end.* That way, we can go ahead and be grappling in now-time with the kinds of questions we know we'll be asking ourselves as we grow older.

I've yet to meet anyone who, when they reach the end of their lives, hopes to find that they wasted their years, hours, and moments. Deep inside, we all want to make a mark here on Earth with the time God has given us. We all want to matter. We all want to be a woman who lived her days well. We all want to be a woman who hears God say, "Well done, my good and faithful servant" when our days here are over. We all want to be faithful women.

That's why, almost more than anything else in my life right now, I love being one of the people talking straight into your ear, telling you how doable, how attainable this goal can be for you. I love being that friend of yours who cheers you on as we journey there together, showing you the truth about who you are and who God is, based on what His Word says.

This desire of mine for being a cheerleader to other women actually goes back a ways. I've known for more than a decade that something inside me wanted to encourage people toward living bigger lives, thinking more deeply about their passions, and then *going* for them, looking long and hard at the talents God had given them and then putting them to work.

I used to blog, for instance. I'm thinking lots of us could probably list that experience as part of our résumés. At first, when I was living a few states away from my parents, blogging was mostly just a tool for keeping my mom and dad in the loop with what was happening with our kids. I'd write funny stories and share pictures that would make my guys blush now if they saw them—you know, like the picture where a little boy was potty training and was constantly wearing his underwear backward? That's the cutest thing on a two-year-old. Not sure why all of us moms were comfortable posting pics of our kids in the Spiderman undies, but whatever.

IveyFamily.blogspot.com. You could've looked it up but, thankfully for my kids' sake, I don't think that page is around anymore.

At one point, after our family began the adoption process for our two kids from Haiti, I updated my blog and gave it a new look, as well as a new name, because I now had a new message to share. I was dreaming big dreams—DreamingBigDreams.com—and I wanted to share those big dreams of our new journey and endeavor with everybody who chose to read about it.

Now that I think about it, not much has changed since that time. This book you're reading is full of those same messages. I want so much for you to chase your dreams and do big things because I am confident big things are awaiting us all. I believe you have world-changing abilities inside you, that your ideas are truly worth something, and that you should pursue your dreams as far as they will take you.

I say all of this, however, with one huge caveat.

You've probably heard and seen these sayings pop up in your Pinterest feed, the things people put out there to motivate and inspire us.

- Girl, you got this.
- You're enough.
- Hustle more.
- Get things done.
- Pick yourself up by your bootstraps.

- You can do anything you put your mind to.
- You control your destiny.
- You are your own boss.

All of these ideas are good. They're super motivating. But I'd like to suggest they're lacking. They are shallow and unsustainable. Not one of them is capable of bringing lasting hope and peace to your life. Not one of them is powerful enough to help you overcome whatever real-life struggle you're facing. I'll even go far enough out on the ledge to proclaim that these truths alone can be damning. Notice I said, "these truths *alone*." Most of them are not entirely bad in themselves. In fact I've probably said them all to different people at various points in my life. But what I'm seeing today is a world where women of faith are taking these cute little sayings and standing on them as if they were the way and the truth and the life.

They're not.

That's the danger in these sayings. They can't hold up under the pressures of the world. Because, no, you're *not* enough, girl. You *ain't* got this. You *can't* hustle enough, can't get enough things done. You *can't* do everything you set your mind on, no matter how badly you want to do it. You *don't* control your own destiny, because the One who made you has the days of your life already numbered, planned, and written for you. And sometimes, life can be so hard that there aren't enough bootstraps in all the world to pull yourself up with. Know what I mean? Yes, I think deep down you know what I mean.

We are only enough because Jesus is enough. The only good things coming from you and me are coming from the Father.

So when I say *You Be You*, understand I'm not just spouting a cheap shout-out. I'm saying YOU have a strength of calling that originates in the mind of God.

> **We are only enough because Jesus is enough.**

I'm saying YOU have a voice and platform that matters immensely today simply because it's the voice He's given you. I'm saying YOU have talents and giftings that He's invested in you, designed for a purpose way bigger than yourself. I'm saying YOU can be defiantly, biblically assured that no trial, no tragedy is oppressive enough to suffocate what He's put you on this earth for.

And this means YOU can experience satisfaction today. YOU can experience success today. Real satisfaction, real success, comes from doing what YOU do, doing it where YOU are, and doing it in faithfulness to the God who has lovingly, strategically put YOU there.

I realize things may look different than you imagined them being at this time in your life. It may not feel as satisfying as you'd hoped, not as satisfying as life seems to be for the people you're constantly comparing yourself against. But that's because of how easily we confuse satisfaction and success with a pretend, phantom lifestyle that doesn't really exist.

I think we have been asking ourselves the wrong questions about our lives. Instead of asking, "Did I do enough today?" what if we asked ourselves, "Did I become more like Jesus today?" Instead of asking, "Was I successful?" what if we asked, "Was I faithful?" Less about us and more about Him. Less about accomplishments and more about our hearts. Less about my glory and more of His glory. Less about comparing our life to *their* lives, and more about comparing our faithfulness to His calling on *our* lives.

I really, truly believe you can do more than you think you can. I believe it's possible to come to the end of your days and be absolutely certain, all the way into your bones, that your life mattered. That you made a difference. That you did the best with what God gave you. That you became more like Him that day. That your striving wasn't for yourself but for a greater purpose than your own.

> **You can do it—because God Himself has already put it there inside you.**

And this book is me being your cheerleader, promising you that you can live out God's will for your life, no matter what season you're in, no matter how your days are looking right now.

You can do it—because God Himself has already put it there inside you.

———

I'm in my forties now, and I love it. I almost feel like Will Ferrell in the movie *Elf*, when he yells, "I'm in love, I'm in love, and I don't care who knows it!" Except I want to yell, "I'm forty, I'm forty, and—" Seriously, I think forty is awesome, and I'm giddy with excitement for what the next decade of my life holds.

I remember so clearly my mom turning forty because my grandmother helped me throw a surprise party for her. We bought "over the hill" signs and stuff and acted as though we were planning more of a funeral than a birthday party. I remember thinking my mom was SO OLD. I had no way to imagine ever being that age. And yet here I am.

Let's say I do live to be eighty, which is roughly the current life expectancy for a woman in America today. I'm not taking eighty for granted, of course. But using that math, I've got about half my life still to go. And I believe these years are going to be great compared to the forty that led up till now.

Because if I'm being super honest, I only count about twenty of those first forty years as being worth anything. (I don't really mean that. Every experience I've gone through is all part of the story that makes my life today, and your life today, the testimony of God's grace that it is.) But, man, does it ever feel sometimes like I wasted mine.

Frankly, the years from twenty to thirty weren't all that exciting for me either, because I spent a lot of that time wishing for things I didn't have. I'll tell you more about this later, but I squandered a lot of my twenties resenting that I was at home with my babies while my husband was traveling the world leading people in worship.

Maybe that's why I love meeting women today in their twenties who are just killing it—the ones who are chasing God hard, listening to Him, leaning into His plans for them. It makes me so happy, seeing this young generation of Christ-followers coming up behind. Because for me, I was around thirty before I finally began living with this idea of making it all count, of living for something bigger than myself. The ideas I write about in this book were not really formed in me until then.

That's what's so beautiful to me about being forty—because basically, I'm only about ten years or so into thinking differently about my life, seeing myself more closely, I believe, to the way *God* thinks about me. And now I've got forty whole years ahead of me (or *one* year, whatever He's planned for me) to completely pour myself out for Him and others, for everyone around me.

And I am so excited about that. It's why I can hardly type fast enough to get everything down I want to say to you because I'm so eager to help you dive deeply into the right-here, right-now calling that God has on your life. Encouraging you today just fires me up—helping you think deeply about all the places you've been, all the stories that you alone can share, all the giftings you have to offer, and how God can transform your whole life when you start seeing all these things through the lens of the gospel.

You can do this! You can show up for the life that God has already ordained for you. You have nothing—nothing!—to lose. Everything to gain. It is *your* day now, my friend—your day, your place, to live the kind of life that you and others can look back on and say, "She used her days well. She was faithful to the end." I so want that person to be me. And I have a small suspicion you want it for yourself as well.

Join me on this journey of becoming women who cease striving to become someone we're not and simply rest in the work that our true hero, Jesus, has already accomplished for us.

Part I

Discovering Yourself

Chapter 2

Faithfulness Comes First

Living Your Calling

One particular summer will forever be etched in my memory—the summer when God asked us to step out in faith and trust Him, the summer when He called us as His children into something new and beautiful with Him.

Do you have a season like that? A season that you will forever look back on and see God's hand all over it as you navigated something new or something big? Or even something awful?

My husband called me one Saturday afternoon while he and my three sons were away on a dude trip to Marfa, Texas, a windswept expanse of wide-open spaces, way out west of our home in Austin. My boys love dude trips, and I've tried to invite myself and my daughter to every single one. But they often remind me that if we came along, it would turn into a family trip, making it no longer a dude trip, and would mess up their whole mojo. So I concede to their dude logic, and we girls go do our own thing while they're gone.

Anyway, I was home when he called, and I could tell right away it was more than a routine check-in to see how we were doing. Something was in the air that he needed to share with me.

A friend of his—someone both of us respect and admire—had spoken with him by phone earlier that morning. It's someone Aaron has done ministry with for years who'd recently relocated to a new city where he and his wife were leading a new church plant.

Cutting to the chase, he offered Aaron a job. With him.

Immediately as he said this to me, my heart sank in my chest, even as I physically sank in my chair. I thought to myself, *A new job? Why would he be asking Aaron if he wanted a new job? Aaron HAS a great job.*

But as he continued to talk to me and explain things further, I could tell why the thought of it was worth considering. God softened my heart to the possibility of us leaving everything we loved, everything we'd helped build, to start over in a new city. He was inviting my husband into something fresh and uncharted, an opportunity to build something new that we believed would be important for this time, and impactful in that place.

Over the next three months, we sought God diligently about our future. We did the pros-and-cons thing. We dreamed about living in a new city, a new house, a new community, all while still loving our community, our home, our church, our city, and our life that we were currently living. Yet it seemed evident that God was indeed moving our hearts toward this new church family. We believed in their mission and the things they were doing. We respected all the pastors involved, and we began to see how we could fit with the church.

Six weeks after Aaron received that initial phone call, we took a quick thirty-hour trip there and saw it with our own eyes. We visited the church and fell instantly in love. We drove around the neighborhood where we imagined ourselves living. We drove by the schools that our kids would attend if this all came to fruition.

Boarding the plane for home at the end of our whirlwind trip, we looked at each other and knew God was indeed calling us to this new church. But we committed to praying and seeking God for another week before we made our final decision.

At the end of that week, it was clear. God was moving us on to a new chapter in our lives.

This was the biggest thing He had ever asked us to do thus far in our marriage and ministry. Despite how happy we were, living our current life, we couldn't help but see God gently and graciously asking us to follow Him anywhere. So we answered yes to this calling, certain that sacrificing what we loved would be worth it for what God had for us.

Then came the weeping.

I wept over leaving the home that had become so dear to me. Then I would weep because of how awful I felt for being so sad about an earthly home.

I wept over the fact that I was certain we were ruining our kids' lives by relocating them to a new city in such formative years. Then I would weep over being sad about asking my kids to do hard things in life.

I wept over my friends, and on and on and on.

A few weeks later, the day finally came for Aaron to do what he'd been dreading throughout this whole process: tell the team he loved so much that he was leaving them to follow where Jesus was calling him.

This would go down as the hardest day of his life so far in his forty years. These men were his teammates. These pastors had poured out their lives alongside Aaron for our church for so many years. And now he was telling them he was leaving to go pour out his life for another church. This hadn't just been any old job; this was our life. We loved our church. We believed in our church. Aaron had overseen a beautiful season of growth and deepening within the worship and creative ministries. It didn't make sense to us why this season needed to end, but we believed God wouldn't call us to something new and not equip us to leave the old one well.

The day when Aaron was informing the other pastors about his decision, I was traveling home from California, praying like crazy for every single meeting (all seven of them) that I knew he would endure during the day. I prayed for every man he would talk to—prayed they would see God's will all over our decision; prayed that Aaron would feel confident in what God was asking us to do; prayed that when we both arrived home that night, we'd be able to recount how God had gone before Aaron in those meetings and prepared hearts to hear what he was saying.

We met back up that night and, to be honest, the confidence we'd each experienced in the weeks leading up to this event was shaky. We were confused. More confused than we'd felt just twenty-four hours earlier, despite our having no doubt that God had called us to this new church. And there was no doubt we would follow Him. We were excited about what was ahead, even though we were dreading the sorrow we would endure to get there.

But as we lay in bed, breathing in and out a new sense of conflict we couldn't explain, we prayed a bold prayer together. One of us prayed that God would speak to us clearly before morning about what He wanted us to do, and the other prayed that God would even show up in our dreams that night to tell us. Then we went to sleep, weary from the emotional strain.

I'll admit, I closed my eyes that night not really knowing what to expect, not really expecting anything from God on such short notice. I've never asked Him to show up in my dreams, and honestly I thought it a bit crazy to ask Him, even as we prayed it. I did know our confidence was gone that evening and our cry in that prayer was a cry of desperation. We wanted God to give us that confidence back. And we wanted it, like, *now*.

When I awoke the next morning, Aaron was already up and moving. And even before I went looking for him, I couldn't shake the feeling that I'd dreamed something totally weird in the night, though I didn't know if it was God's answer-to-prayer dream, like we'd asked for, or just a crazy Tylenol PM dream.

Aaron looked a little pained when I found him, as if his heart and soul were in a battle and I honestly wasn't sure who was winning. He said he'd been up for a while, but in the last thirty minutes he'd been hearing the same phrase over and over in his head, as if someone was audibly speaking to him on a continuous loop.

But before he told me what it was, he asked if I'd dreamed anything. *Yes,* I said. Several dreams actually, and they were all fairly crazy. But one of them stood out to me that I couldn't seem to shake. It felt important and kooky all at the same time.

In my dreams that night, I had pictured myself at a church service. I was on the front row. I don't know who was preaching. But whoever it was, the preacher spoke to me in the service, telling me to look inside my daughter's red homework folder which was underneath the seat I was sitting in. In my dream I could see myself opening up a red folder, and inside of it was one sheet of paper, with only one word written on it.

STAY

As I said this out loud to Aaron, we both began to realize God had indeed shown up in my dream and spoken to us just like we had prayed and asked Him to do. I admit I almost couldn't believe this. God had never spoken to me in a dream before.

Aaron then began to tell me what *he'd* been hearing from God that morning: a single phrase, repeated again and again, from the moment he'd woken up.

I'm not done.
WAIT.

Over and over, like a broken record.
I'm not done. Wait.

We didn't exactly know what to make of this, except that we knew what we'd prayed, and we knew what had happened to each of us in the night. But if I didn't know any better—even though we'd already committed to the new church by this time and had plane tickets for the following weekend to go look at houses and schools and the church with our whole family—it seemed like He'd shown up and told us to stay.

Aaron left early for the day. And with the house still quiet, I thought I'd go peek in my daughter's backpack to see if a red homework folder was in there. I pulled out about eight different binders, all different colors, and only a single red one. Starting with every binder that wasn't red, I opened them all up. There wasn't one piece of paper inside of any of them. (She'd been in school for two days. Had they given her nothing to put in her folders?)

I then opened the red one—the only folder that had any paper inside of it. And clear as day on her syllabus for that class were the following bold letters at the top of the page:

STAY

Tears. God had shown up in our dreams, just as we'd asked Him. And He'd showed up in my heart that morning through a red homework folder in my daughter's room.

He had asked us to go to a new city; we had followed Him and said yes.

Now He was asking us to stay; and we would be faithful to that as well. By saying yes again.

By being faithful to His calling.

———

I'm going to make a bold statement, and I hope it frees you up as much as it's done for me.

If you are a follower of Jesus, you and I have the same ultimate calling: *to make Him known and bring Him glory.*

That's it. End of story.

Can you breathe a sigh of relief then? God will call you and me to a hundred or more things throughout our lifetimes, but our one primary calling will never change. It will never be smaller or larger. It will always be what He asks of each of us: living our lives in a way that *makes Him known and brings Him glory.*

And here's what I've found over the years in terms of this highest calling from God. We will fulfill this calling when we decide to faithfully follow Him day by day no matter where He takes us. No special messages or long seasons of deliberation over whether we're hearing Him right or misreading His direction. Just be faithful. Faithful where we are. Faithful to His Word.

As Christ-followers, we have been commissioned by Jesus Himself to go out and make disciples, to tell those around us how He has changed our lives and what the Father offers to them as well. Jesus' final words before ascending to heaven tell us to do just that.

> "Go therefore and make disciples of all
> nations, baptizing them in the name of the
> Father and of the Son and of the Holy Spirit,

teaching them to observe all that I have com-
manded you. . . ."

In leaving to go back to the Father after His death and
resurrection, Jesus' charge to His disciples was to go make
more disciples in His name, to make known their saving God
to everyone they met.

And this same command and charge are still in place
for us today. No matter what decisions you make in living
out your calling—no matter where you move or where you
stay—you have an ultimate calling on your life to make Him
known. It doesn't begin when you get out of college, or get a
job, or get married, or have kids, or start a ministry. It begins
when you follow Jesus.

Throughout this book, we're going to talk about how we
walk out our callings amid trials and tragedy. We're going to
look at what God asks us to do with our gifts and talents.
We're going to examine what it looks like to fight for contentment in our lives and to cheer on others around us. My
prayer and hope for all of us is that as our gifts and talents
come alive, and as we go to the places God asks us to go, and
as we follow Him to the ends of the earth, we would realize
our good works are meant for one thing and one thing only:
to bring Him glory.

Nothing else. No glory for us. No glory for our churches.
No glory for our organizations. God and God alone deserves
the glory. And when we are faithful wherever we are and

making Him known however we can, He gets a crazy amount of glory. The glory He deserves.

In one of my favorite set of verses from the Sermon on the Mount, Jesus says:

> "You are the light of the world. A city set on a hill cannot be hidden. Nor do people light a lamp and put it under a basket, but on a stand, and it gives light to all in the house. In the same way, let your light shine before others, so that they may see your good works and give glory to your Father who is in heaven."

Our good works, our gifts, our talents, our *whole lives* are meant to shine His light on others so that they may give glory to our Father. Our ultimate, highest calling is to make Him known and bring Him glory.

So whenever I use the word "calling" from now on as we journey together through this book, I will not be talking about our ultimate calling, our BIG calling. We've established what that is. We've laid that groundwork. I'll be talking instead about the individual callings that over time make up your faithful Christian life. Your YOU callings. Your specifically personal callings.

My friend and author Rebekah Lyons states that your calling is where your "talents and burdens collide." What has God put on your heart as a burden? What gifts and talents has He given you? This intersection is often where we see God moving and calling us into new things.

I have another friend who often says, "The need is the call." I love everything about that. What if we viewed our callings this way? What if we looked around and saw needs, and then looked at ourselves and saw gifts, talents, passions, and proximity, and decided we would meet those needs with what's already been put in our hands?

I can give you a personal example from one of the first times Aaron and I felt "called" to something specific and unexplainable.

We'd recently packed up our lives from Texas and headed out to Tennessee so that Aaron could continue making music and traveling the country leading people in worship. We were so young, had so little money between our two ragtag careers, and to top it off, had found ourselves starting a family so much sooner than we'd planned.

I had begun working at a homeschool co-op—a collection of like-minded families who bring their kids together for classes. I was teaching middle school English one day a week,[1] which was a real godsend for me. I was able to teach, which is what I'd been doing before we moved, was able to pour into students' lives, be around people, AND (best of all)

---

[1] My degree is in kinesiology, the study of movement, which is nowhere close to English. (I was a coach and teacher before we had kids.) If I taught your child in one of these English classes, I'd like to offer you a full refund.

take my new baby to work with me. Not much money, but to me—great benefits.

While working there, I met a woman named Gwen, another one of the moms who taught at the co-op. What struck me about Gwen from the beginning was that she seemed so full of life and energy. I loved being around her. And not long after meeting her, I found out that she and her husband were adopting a little girl from China.

Adopting? I don't think I'd ever met anyone at that point in my life who was seeking to adopt. At least no one that I could remember. The whole idea sounded like the craziest thing to me. But I kept listening to her story about what led them to adopt and how the process was going.

Over the next few months, I met more and more people in our church who were also adopting. Another couple was adopting from China as well, who introduced me to more of their friends who were also adopting. It seemed as though overnight we were surrounded by people who were in the process of expanding their family through adoption—something totally new to Aaron and me, and yet suddenly, it was everywhere we looked.

Was God calling us to adoption?

Over those months, we began seeking God about it, listening for Him, then eventually walking this calling out. We stepped out in faith and asked Him to guide us forward into whatever He desired for us. We yearned to be in step with

Him, not wanting to miss one single thing He had in store for us.

Our *big* calling was still the same. It always is. But adoption became for us, in God's way of dealing individually with us, an underlying part of our overall calling.

And He does the same with you. With *all* His kids. With *all* our specific callings.

But here's where it gets tricky, right? How do we *know* what God's calling is? Like with Aaron and me and the ordeal we went through in trying to determine whether God was calling us to move that summer—Was it yes? Was it no? We heard God ask us to lay it all down for a new adventure with Him. Then at the last moment, we heard Him ask us to lay down the new adventure and stay where we'd been.

The first week after this happened, I had a small crisis of faith. I felt like I had missed God all summer. I was the one who'd been the most confident in this calling from God since the get-go. I had hardly wavered in thinking I knew where He was asking us to go. Aaron dug in deep and fought it out with God, but I was sure He was calling us to this new church and new journey.

I wondered now if I could hear from God at all. Had I missed Him the whole time? Was there never an ask from Him? I'd been so confident of it that now I felt like a fool. Like I had missed Him. Like maybe I didn't even know Him. (Okay, that last line sounds dramatic as I read it back, but at the very least I was *extremely* confused!)

After much prayer, talking it out, and—yes, some counseling too—God showed me something. He *had* called us to something new. We *hadn't* missed Him. We *could* still hear Him.

We *did* know Him and *do* know Him.

The light bulb went off for me when I recalled the story of Abraham and Isaac from the Old Testament. Starting in Genesis 15, God made a covenant with Abraham that his offspring would outnumber the stars. He promised Abraham and his wife Sarah a son. The only problem was that they were *really* old. Too old to be having their first kid anyway. As in, so old that when God told this news to Abraham, he laughed out loud and said to God, "Shall a child be born to a man who is a hundred years old? Shall Sarah, who is ninety years old, bear a child?"

Guess what? Don't laugh at what God promises. Sarah did indeed get pregnant as God had said, and they became the parents of a son named Isaac—the beloved son that God had promised to Abraham.

That's why when we get to Genesis 22, it all seems so terribly confusing because of what God then asked Abraham to do:

> He said, "Take your son, your only son
> Isaac, whom you love, and go to the land of
> Moriah, and offer him there as a burnt offer-
> ing on one of the mountains of which I shall

tell you." So Abraham rose early in the morning, saddled his donkey, and took two of his young men with him, and his son Isaac. And he cut the wood for the burnt offering and arose and went to the place of which God had told him.

God had promised Abraham that his offspring would be great in number, and now He was asking him to sacrifice the only son that God had given him. It doesn't make sense to us as readers, and I can only imagine that it didn't make much sense to Abraham, Sarah, and Isaac either.

But if you've been in church long enough, you know the ending of the story. They journeyed to the place where God instructed him to sacrifice Isaac. Abraham collected the wood needed for the burnt offering, built an altar, bound up his son, and laid him on it. Then just as Abraham raised his knife in the air to strike his son, an angel of the Lord called out to him, stopped the sacrifice, and provided a ram in a thicket for him to sacrifice instead.

I've read and heard that story a hundred times, and not once in all the times I heard it did I ever think Abraham misunderstood God. Never. I've never heard a message preached, or read a commentary, or thought as I was reading it that Abraham somehow lost his ability to hear from God and made a mistake, that he heard wrong when he thought God was telling him to sacrifice his son.

Abraham *had* heard from God. God *had* called him to make that sacrifice. He *had* asked Abraham to follow Him into the unknown, to do the impossible, and Abraham trusted and loved God so much that he knew God would keep His word to him. He believed his offspring would outnumber the stars, no matter how unlikely this promise seemed if he followed up on this highly unexpected change of plans.

Abraham just decided to be faithful, no matter what.

And I guess that's what Aaron and I had done, too, to the best of our ability. God had asked us to move to another city and pour our lives into a new church, and we said yes. Then God asked us to stay, and we said yes to that as well.

And I just think that's the secret. By choosing first to be *faithful,* even amid the frequent uncertainties of exactly what God may be calling you to do, that's how you stay true to your calling. You will glorify Him and make Him super proud as long as your heart beats every day to be faithful to Him, to make Him known in every way you possibly can.

Lots of freedom in that.

———

Let me address a soapbox of mine quickly, since we're talking about callings. Do you mind? It's my book, so I guess I can really do whatever I want.

Here goes: Your highest calling in life is not marriage or motherhood.[2] God may indeed have called you to these things, but they are not your *highest* calling.

My friend and author Kat Armstrong, in her book *No More Holding Back*, says, "Dethroning the idols of Christian marriage and motherhood does not in any way devalue the institution of marriage or family. It elevates God to his unrivaled throne." We have done a disservice to many women in our churches by making them feel, either by our words or our actions, that marriage and motherhood are the *ultimate* indicators of godliness. I see many women today throwing away the passions and talents that God has given them because they've bought the lie that the ONLY thing they're good for is being a wife and a mom.

Now don't hear me saying marriage and motherhood are not high callings. *They are.* They're wonderful. I'm beyond grateful for my own marriage and family. But let's think for a second. If we elevate marriage and motherhood to the pre-eminent calling on EVERY woman, where does that leave the women in your lives who are not wives or mothers?

It's just not true. It will never be true. If you're a woman reading this, you need to know that God has called you to big things even if you're *not* a mom or a wife. Neither one of those things is a woman's universal qualification for changing the world, doing ministry, or glorifying God with her life.

---

[2] "Parenthood," if you're a man reading this.

I am both of these things, both a wife and a mom, and I'm terrifically proud of it. But I can say without hesitation that my highest calling in life was not found when I said "I do" to Aaron or pushed out my first child.[3]

Big calling? Yes.

The biggest? No.

Let me turn it around for you though. If you're a mom devoting the majority of your hours to your kids during this season of life, the message is not that one calling is better. Being where God wants you is always best. Your faithfulness is being right where God has you. All I'm saying is this: your ministry, your gifts, and the way God plans on using you do not start, OR END, with marriage or motherhood.

> **Being where God wants you is always best.**

Okay, I'm off my soapbox now.

Thank you. I do feel better.

But I still know discerning your calling is something that may be keeping you up at night with worry and impatience, wondering if you might have missed it, wondering if you can even hear God for it. As I've shared with you in this chapter, I was a grown woman wading through all those fears that summer, so I have a feeling you may be experiencing this same

---

[3] Which I feel the need to tell you: the one and only child of mine to whom I gave physical birth was a whopping 9 pounds, 11 ounces!

kind of thing right now, or you've experienced it in the past, or you'll experience it again soon.

Do you want to know my entire goal for this book? I'm letting you in on it now, and hopefully by the time you get to the end you'll feel what I'm about to tell you.

I want you to do what God has
equipped you to do with the passions
and talents He's put inside you.

I want you to show up for your life. I want you to believe and trust that He has good things for you, and that He wants to use you to do big things right where you are. I want you convinced that you'll make the greatest impact on your world when you allow Him to work through you right where He's planted you.

I want you to be you.

Living your calling.

Which simply means being faithful. Not being super smart. Not being a spiritual giant. Not always knowing the answer to every question or feeling completely in control of every situation.

Just faithful. To Him. Where you are. With what you know. With what you have.

The calling on Aaron's and my life to relocate was real. The calling on our lives to add to our family through adoption was also real. Doesn't mean we opened the Bible one day and saw the words: "Aaron and Jamie, go adopt three kids."

Doesn't mean we were given chapter and verse about relocating our family to a new city and a new church. Absolutely not. I so wish that's what had happened, but it didn't. It just doesn't.

But as I look back on these major decisions in our lives, I do see a few things we did that helped us discern His calling. And if you're someone who's trying to determine where He's directing you right now, I hope these four observations from our experience are helpful to you.

1. Be in the Word.

Much too often, I think, people try to figure out what God has called them to do without spending any time with Him. We expect Him to reveal things to us even though we're not really investing into the relationship. But the Bible says if we want to know the will of God, we need our minds thinking the way God thinks. And the only way to do that is by keeping our ears open to what He says. By staying rooted in His Word.

I grew up in a culture that taught if you weren't having a daily quiet time with God, you weren't a good Christian. And while I completely agree with the importance of maintaining this spiritual discipline, the habit of spending time with Him can become, if we're not careful, a box that we know we should check instead of something we look forward to doing.

This kind of religious nonsense has changed for me through the years. No longer am I concerned merely about doing things a "good Christian" does. My desire is to know God. To know Him more. To know Him better. Because until we truly want to know Him by hearing Him speak to us through His Word, we shouldn't expect Him to tell us much.

The Bible is a "light" to our path. It is "living and active." Its truths have been "breathed out" by God Himself. And those who discover what He's calling them to do are those who keep their minds renewed by His Word on an ongoing basis. "Do not be conformed to this world," Paul said, "but be transformed by the renewal of your mind, that by testing you may discern what is the will of God, what is good and acceptable and perfect." Time spent in the Word is monumental if we want to know and discern what God intends to accomplish through us.

2. Listen to the Holy Spirit.

If you're a follower of Jesus, I have the best news for you right now! You have a Helper who goes with you everywhere you go, enabling you to know God more, make Him known, and ascertain the next step He wants you taking in life.

When Jesus was hanging out with His disciples for what would be the last time they'd see Him before His crucifixion, He told them He was leaving them, that He was going to His Father. I'm pretty sure they were confused and probably freaking out over all this. They wanted their friend and teacher to stay with them. We'd feel the same way.

But it wouldn't be the end. In fact, as hard as it would have been for them to believe Him in that moment, Jesus said His Father was going to be giving them something that would make their lives even better.

> "I will ask the Father, and he will give you another Helper, to be with you forever, even the Spirit of truth, whom the world cannot receive, because it neither sees him nor knows him. You know him, for he dwells with you and will be in you."

This "Helper," He said, "will teach you all things and bring to your remembrance all that I have said to you."

Which is just what we need, right? I can't even believe sometimes the gift that God has given us in the Holy Spirit, living right here inside us, enlightening us, helping us. As Jesus went on to say:

> "When the Spirit of truth comes, he will guide you into all the truth, for he will not speak on his own authority, but whatever he hears he will speak, and he will declare to you the things that are to come. He will glorify me, for he will take what is mine and declare it to you."

The Holy Spirit is our guide. Our helper. Our truth. And we need to be listening for Him—listening in prayer, listening in worship, listening to His Word—listening, listening, listening. Part of what makes discerning God's calling difficult for us is when we're flooded by more input and information than we think we can handle. Our thoughts can even *compete* with one another, leaving us totally confused about which way we should go. That's how we get caught up in wanting God to just come out and tell us, almost like a big HGTV home renovation reveal.

And yet God has sent Someone to help guide us, show us the truth, and speak to us from His heart . . . if we'll only listen to Him.

3. Surround yourself with a solid community.

Another huge contributor to discerning your calling is the wisdom found in community. I'd even say it's absolutely vital. Making tough decisions is hard, even when we invite trusted friends into the conversation, but *nothing's* as hard as trying to do it purely on our own steam, with no one else listening or weighing in or counseling us with their input.

Not just any kind of community is up to this task, however. Even if we get past our desire to stay private and insulated, we sometimes only seek out other people who are similar to us, people who'll be more likely to agree with us or tell us what we want to hear.

So when I talk about surrounding yourself with community, I'm talking about *solid* community. People who won't just pat you on the back but will push you to think. People who won't just pay you compliments but will make sure you're hearing the truth, whether cheerful or challenging. People who are really there, in flesh and blood, right beside you in close proximity, not just advice givers on Instagram who can't really hold you accountable. And maybe most important, people from different age groups, different life stages, people who come at life from different perspectives and can shine a light on those things that tend to hide in your blind spots.

Your church certainly ought to be a primary place for you to locate this kind of solid community. You need to be interacting with people who understand your big calling for making God known and bringing Him glory. But you'll find them in other places too, from family and friends to like-minded gatherings of other people. Allow them to speak into your life about what they see as your giftings and passions. See if they affirm the same things you're sensing. Or not. I know it's sometimes hard to bring people into our junk, to open up to that extent, but I'll say it in every book I ever write and from every stage I ever stand on. *We Are Better Together!*

4. Live your life openhanded.

Aaron and I have lived our entire marriage with our hands opened to the Lord. What I mean is that we are 100 percent sold out to where we are, and we are 100 percent open to wherever God might want us to be. Which makes for the best life of all. When you live out your gifts, talents, and passions 100 percent, you allow yourself to go and be exactly where and who God wants you to be. It takes the fear out of wondering if you're in the right place because you'd go there in a second if that's where He pointed you.

This approach to life has been beautiful for our family. It's allowed us to serve Him faithfully and be open to wherever He would send us. It's what has led our family on every crazy journey we've ever embarked on.

Openhanded living, for me, means I'm going to devote every ounce of dedication to my current job. Right now this calling is podcasting, speaking, and writing, each of which I truly love. It brings me so much joy using my gifts here where God wants me to be. But I also hold my hands open to whatever God calls me to do, which might be something that looks different than what I'm doing now. God might ask me to let something go. He might ask me to pivot and do something else.

I understand if this feels scary to you. I'd suggest to you, though, God means for it to bring you comfort, knowing you don't need to live your life constantly looking for the next big thing, constantly dreaming about what could be. You can simply be committed and devoted to what's in front of you, even while allowing Him to move or adjust those things as He pleases. It's all so very freeing, I think.

On a personal level, openhanded living had me knee-deep in motherhood for many, many years, pouring out my life into the season I was currently occupying. Did I already have talents and gifts for other things, the kinds of things He'd call me to do in the future? For sure. But was it time for my calling to shift

> **You don't need to live your life constantly looking for the next big thing . . . You can simply be committed and devoted to what's in front of you.**

toward using them in a more full-time way? Not yet. I didn't create my first podcast until I was thirty-six. I didn't become a public speaker or release my first book until I was almost forty.

But again, it's all about faithfulness. Being faithful to God in the here and now, while remaining free to not worry about what it means to be faithful in the future.

It's beautiful. It's great.

You should try it. You'll love it.

Listening to God and hearing His call on your life is something that should never grow old to us. As you do it with things that seem small in your life, as well as with things that feel like they're the biggest decision you'll ever make, you'll want to stay tethered to His Word, listen to what the Spirit says to you, involve your community, and keep your hands held open at all times.

I tell you all this to remind you, when you think of God's calling (not your BIG calling but your YOU calling), think of it as an ever-changing cycle of listening, learning, and moving. God called Aaron and me to adopt, then He called us to move to Austin, then He eventually called us to lay everything down in Austin and move to a new church community, before calling us back at the last minute to stay put and keep serving Him right where we'd been. It has kept changing and developing. None of it has been easy. But I wouldn't want to have missed a single day of it.

So, what is your calling? That's what you want to know, isn't it? You want me to tell you the twelve steps to knowing your calling and thriving in it. Are you called to adopt like us? Are you called to a pastoral ministry like us? Are you called to live overseas? Are you called to grow your YouTube show? Are you called to singleness? Are you called to teach in the inner city? Are you called to go to medical school? Are you called to _____? Fill in the blank. We're all asking the same questions.

You're called to be faithful.

And God will fill in the rest.

Life will throw you curveballs. You'll walk through the hardest seasons ever. Your career will change. You'll yearn for marriage a lot longer than you ever imagined. Sickness and death will enter your world unexpectedly. Your marriage will get hard. Your passions will grow and diminish over time.

But in every circumstance, God will still have a calling for you—a way for you to be you, in Him. And whatever that calling of yours is, the path that takes you there is faithfulness.

> **But in every circumstance, God will still have a calling for you—a way for you to be you, in Him.**

Chapter 3

Your Seat at the Table

Finding Your Voice

In 2011 my entire life changed forever. (Sounds so very dramatic. Let me rephrase.) In 2011 my *career* life changed forever. (Much better, Jamie.) I tend to lean toward dramatic. I can't help it.

Because let's be honest, if I'm going to talk about the years when my life changed forever, I'd better list:

- 1999, when my heart changed forever about Jesus[4]

---

[4] I attended the Passion conference in 1999 and the Holy Spirit did what He does best. My soul was captured forever. I write all about

- 2001, when I married the love of my life
- 2004, when I became a momma for the first time
- 2005, when I became a momma again
- 2009, when I became a momma to my first daughter
- 2010, when my final son joined our family

I feel like a better person when talking about the years that changed my life forever if I include my sweet family in the conversation!

Okay, back to 2011.

At this point in my life, I was a stay-at-home momma who shuffled kids around, took care of the house, and hadn't worked full-time since before I had kids in 2004. I'm fully aware that being a momma with the choice to stay home with my kids was a privilege that many women in our world never have the opportunity to even entertain. I was grateful for it. (Most of the time.) It's just where I was in my life. In 2011.

But I remember the day—remember exactly where I was, taking my kids to Mother's Day Out—when I entertained for the first time the idea of a new career.

---

this experience in my first book, *If You Only Knew,* and although this sounds like a plug to go out and buy my book, it's not. But if you want to go buy it, you can. I'm certainly not here to hold anyone back from reading whatever they choose to read!

I was minding my own business that morning, just driving along, when my local country radio station made an announcement that caused me to turn up the radio and listen a bit closer. They said they were searching for a new addition to their already popular morning show, a position they'd decided to fill by opening it up to a contest. Here's how it would work:

(1) Record a sixty-second demo.

(2) Get friends to vote for you.

Then (3) they pick a winner.

Now maybe you're reading this and thinking, *Yes, I would totally do that too,* while others may be thinking, *Are you kidding? That sounds like the worst thing in the world.* Whenever I tell this story to people, I look in their eyes and can immediately tell which of these two reactions is theirs. They either think exactly like me or completely opposite of me. Two distinct reactions. Always.

To me, I genuinely thought to myself that this idea sounded fabulous and that I had as good a shot at it as anyone else. Did I think I'd win? No. But I thought it'd be fun to try.

The most important thing, however, about this feeling of mine is that when I had it, there was no visible reason why I should feel that way. In 2011, I had no public persona at all. The only people who knew my name were my neighbors, my family, and my friends. I was coming into this contest as a regular ol' stay-at-home mom who had no experience in this field at all. Zero. None. My degrees in college were in kinesiology, like I said, as well as speech communications. Nothing around radio and television. I knew nothing about the job that I was entertaining the idea of auditioning for, except that it sounded fun. And I'm here to say: that's a great reason to apply for a job!

After dropping off the kids, I raced home to tell my husband all about this amazing opportunity that I just knew I should apply for. And to the best of my recollection, the first thing he did was laugh. I don't mean to throw him under the bus here, but he most certainly didn't think I could win. I mean, let's be honest, I wasn't actually qualified for this job I was applying for! He thought my eager ambition was . . . *that's cute, Jamie. You're funny, Jamie.*

In his defense, the only reason he was home at all was because he had the flu that day. To me, though, the main reason it mattered that he was home was so he could help me record my sixty-second demo telling the world why I would be the best girl for the show.

Do you know how hard it is to convince someone who feels like they're knocking on death's door to get up out of bed, walk to their home studio, and help someone make a demo who's never spoken into a microphone before, for a contest the person has no shot at winning? Let me tell you, it is super hard.

But I did it. I mean *he* did it. We recorded what I am most certain sounded like a woman who had no clue what she was doing trying to convince people why they should vote for her. I wish so badly I could find that recording and put the transcript here for us all to laugh at. I don't remember what I said, but I know I put on my best "radio voice" and introduced myself to the city of Austin, Texas, and its country music fans.

Looking back now, I am so proud of that girl. There's nothing that says I should have applied for this position. Nothing in my background said I would be good at it. Nothing. And yet there was something in me that thought it would be a fun job, and I knew I would love it and be good at it if I won.

But if I'm honest with you, I had dreamed of something like this forever. Back when we lived in Tennessee, where I'd delivered our first son and we had brought our second son home from Texas, through a domestic adoption, I'd actually looked for jobs at our local television stations. Aaron at the time was on the road about 250 days a year, leading worship at different youth and college events. He was right where God wanted him—and so was I—but I admit, a lot of days I wondered if there was more to my life than diapers, play-dates, park swings, and Elmo. But none of the jobs those stations were offering were ones I was interested in. I wanted to be the anchor! I wanted to be on-screen, on-camera, not behind the scenes making coffee and writing stories.

I remember feeling as though I wanted to have a *voice* in the world. I wanted to do something that mattered, more than what was happening at my home on the daily.

Understand I'm not *proud* of feeling that way. I hope you'll see as you keep reading how God has worked a lot in my heart on what it means to make an impact, and how the impact we make can look different in the varying stages of our lives. No less valuable, just different.

Nonetheless, I lived at that time with this constant desire for more. I loved my life as a momma. Truly I did. I loved raising my kids. It's not like I was sitting around my house unhappy. But there was always a tug in me that wanted to do more.

I tell you all that to say: when I heard the commercial advertising this contest, it caught me in a moment when my heart was wanting a tad bit more. I don't think it's just that I wanted more, but I felt there was more inside of me. And God's leading me to apply for a job that I had no qualifications for was His first step of moving me toward the "more" He had in mind for me down the road. This opportunity felt like something I could grasp on to and thrive in.

I sent in the demo, and the fun began.

It was a voting contest,[5] and so every day I would get on Facebook and ~~beg~~ remind my friends to go and vote for me. I emailed anyone I could think of, ~~begging~~ asking them

---

[5] I refer to this contest as the "*American Idol* Radio Contest" in Austin.

to vote. It surely didn't hurt my chances that our church of around 2,500 at the time had my back and was on the voting train.

But though all of my friends were voting for me because they loved me, I knew they weren't necessarily doing it because they thought I was the best candidate for the job. I mean, I'm sure they would say I was. But I could still get all those votes, possibly make the top ten, and then the radio executives would hear my demo and disregard me as a potential hire. This thought crossed my mind often, but I would try to dismiss it and keep drumming up votes. I needed to win the fans' approval before I worried about the executives' approval!

And somehow, I was doing it. It was the craziest thing. I was actually on the leaderboard for most of the voting period. Every day I would check and couldn't believe it. It looked like I was going to make the top ten for sure, without a doubt.

It was so much fun.

But was it becoming more than that?

———

As the contest began to come to a close, Aaron and I went out on a date one night. It was the first time we had the "what if" conversation. He looked at me with all sincerity and asked what I thought we would do if I won, if our life actually began involving my working at a radio station as a morning DJ. I mean, it had been all fun and games up to this point, but the results were indicating I had decent odds to get it. What would that look like? We now had four kids at home, and my job was to take care of them every single day. What if I was no longer home for half of it?

Still, it all seemed so unlikely. We giggled at the question, basically laughing it off. There wasn't any real way I was getting this job. Was there?

Well, I don't know—because after what seemed like years of me ~~begging~~ asking my friends for votes, the top ten were finally secured, and my name was number one. I'd made the top ten! OH, MY GOSH! HOW DID THIS HAPPEN? And when the people in charge at the radio station whittled down the entries to the ones they wanted to consider, I MADE THE TOP FIVE!

Unbelievable.

The way it worked from there: each of the five remaining contestants were invited to come in for a morning and be a guest host on the show. Everyone was assigned a day, and my day was Thursday. I felt good about this day because I'd be able to listen to three other contestants go before me in hopes of winning over the team, the executives, and the listeners. I don't think I'd ever been more nervous about anything in my entire life.

I shopped that week for a new outfit, because when you make your debut on the radio, you need to look good! Right? I thought about things we might talk about and tried to be as prepared as I could. I sent a message on Facebook reminding all my friends and fans[6] to tune in, since they were the ones who'd gotten me this opportunity.

Monday, Tuesday, Wednesday all came and went.

Then came Thursday.

I had no idea what traffic would look like at five in the morning, so I was fifteen minutes early for my 6:00 a.m. debut. When I walked into the station, they introduced me to everyone, and the news reporter handed me a paper. Said I might want to read over today's headlines.

Oh, yeah. That would have been a great way to prep for the day, now wouldn't it, instead of shopping for the perfect outfit. I breezed over it quickly, retaining as much as I could. At 6:00, we went live. I was so nervous and excited for whatever the morning would bring!

I left that day truly declaring that if nothing else happened for me as a result of that contest, this day had been worth it all. It had been so much fun! The guys in the studio were so kind and encouraging toward me. They asked great questions and it felt like they truly cared about me as a person. I left the studio that day beaming, wanting this job even more than when I'd walked in that morning.

The station then took forever to pick a winner, and I waited and waited. Dreamed and dreamed about what my life would look like if I started down a new career path.

---

[6] "Fans" is a joke. I had five fans, and they all lived in my house.

Then the phone call came—the one that "changed my life forever." I'm still being dramatic about it, I know, but I seriously point my career back to this moment in my life. The station called, and I was live with them on the radio while they introduced me as the newest member of the KVET morning team. I was standing on my front porch talking to them on the phone while the city of Austin listened and my family cheered me on from the living room. I was beaming with pride.

This girl just got herself a J.O.B.

What happened next was a whirlwind. I had to get childcare in place and figure out how my life would run now that I was working. Not only was my life about to drastically change, but my kids' lives were changing, and my husband's life as well.

Between about five girls, consisting of friends and babysitters, we put a system in place for my kids to be taken care of in my absence. When Aaron was traveling, one of them would arrive at my house at 5:00 a.m. so I could get to work on time. It took a village to keep the Ivey household running.

But this job was my dream job. I loved every minute of it. I felt empowered for the first time in a long time. I felt valued in a way that I hadn't felt before in my lifetime. More important, I felt as

You already have a voice. Where you are. Where you live.

though I had a *voice*—a voice I'd never experienced up until this point in my life.

Looking back though, that's the feeling that haunts me the most to this day. That's why I've taken up all this space inviting you into the drama of my radio-contest adventure. What I was feeling was not a *new* voice, but simply a new avenue for using the voice I'd already been given.

You already have a voice.

Where you are. Where you live.

It wouldn't be long before I'd be teaching myself this same lesson.

———

Everyone has a part to play on a radio team, and I was for sure the goody-goody Christian girl. I was 100 percent fine with playing that part because it didn't feel like a part to me. It was just who I was.

One day I was telling the guys off the air how I'd recently looked through a workout magazine that came to Aaron at the house, and how I'd torn out all the pages that included inappropriate pictures before he got home to read it. I can't adequately explain to you what a little nothing I considered my actions to be. It was as simple and innocent as this: it came in the mail, I randomly flipped through it, tore out a few pages, and placed it back on the counter. No biggie. Really. It's not as though I was in the habit (then or now) of storming around the house, demanding to see what my husband is reading or looking at. The reason I could say it so offhand to my work friends is because that's how offhand I thought the whole thing to be. In fact I'm fairly sure this was the only time I'd ever torn pages out of any magazine, and to be honest, I really have no idea what made me tell that story to them that day.

And yet you'd think I'd just mentioned that I secretly knew who killed JFK. The entire room stopped. Everyone's heads turned toward me in slow motion as they demanded more information about this magazine page-ripping thing I'd confessed to committing. *It was NOTHING,* I said. It's just that I couldn't believe some of the photos that were in there, and I was helping keep my man and my kids pure by tearing out the pages that I thought they didn't need to see.

All they heard, though, was a woman trying to control her husband as if he were a twelve-year-old boy. *And* they heard the spark of an idea that we could talk about on-air. "Did I mind?" they asked.

No. But I had no idea what I was getting myself into when I agreed to retell this story for the listening public. I shared with the guys what I'd shared with them a few days earlier (you know, as if we'd never talked about it before), and they expressed their confusion even more than they'd done in private. They played it up big. Now to their credit they never made me look like a weirdo or a bad wife by the questions they asked. They were genuinely just dumbfounded that this was even a thing. To them it seemed odd that I would even care what my husband looked at, much less cut out pages from his magazines.

It was nuts what came my way. The phones blew up. The emails started rolling in. The Facebook comments went crazy. I was now officially a controlling wife to most listeners. They couldn't believe my husband loved me if I would do something so stalkerish as this. Listeners called in to tell me they were certain my husband was looking at porn on the daily since I was keeping him from these photos in the magazine.

I was shocked—shocked by the onslaught of women and men berating me for my values.

At one point the host of the show called my husband and asked him questions about it on-air. Aaron responded like a champ, and I think we were able to demonstrate a marriage that was built on mutual trust and our care for the purity of each other's hearts.

But I learned something that day I've never forgotten. No matter where you are in your life, when you get the opportunity to speak up against something that you know is not right or is dishonoring to God, people will oppose you, attack your character, or try to silence you. But I was encouraged to hear in my voice what I considered to be the fruit of the Spirit—the voice of a woman who valued her marriage and her morals, the voice of a woman who believed that God had a purpose for me.

I truly loved the voice I discovered. I discovered my voice mattered.

Like yours does. Like everyone's does.

———

God seems to go out of His way in Scripture to show us women who spoke up for what mattered to them, who used their voices for influential purposes. Despite the fact that they lived in a time and culture where women were thought to have *no* voice, they overcame their fear and insecurity and said what needed to be said.

When Aaron and I were considering adopting from Haiti, and I imagined adopting a little girl from there, I wanted to name her Esther because of the story I love about Queen Esther in the Bible. The Bible story itself is inspiring enough on its own, of course, though there's nothing like watching VeggieTales[7] reenact Queen Esther! I used to love watching it with my kids. The premise is the same as the story in the Bible, except in the real story the bad guy was hanged, and in the video he's sent to the Island of Perpetual Tickling. Much more family-friendly, I assume.

If you don't know the story of Esther, I'll summarize it for you really quick. Esther was adopted by her cousin Mordecai

———

[7] A video series where vegetables act out Bible stories. Sounds weird, but trust me, kids love it!

because she had no other family. They were living their normal life when the king of Persia—King Ahasuerus—got rid of his wife because she didn't respect him. True story, you can read it for yourself. Then his officials suggested that he bring in many beautiful women so that he could choose a new wife. These women spent twelve months getting beauty treatments. (I love a beauty treatment just as much as the next girl, but twelve months is a lot!) Eventually the king chose Esther. Sounds like a modern-day "Housewives of Persia" episode, if you ask me!

What Esther didn't tell anyone, however, not even her new hubby the king, was that she was Jewish—an oversight that became more important when one of the king's main officials decided he wanted all the Jews murdered, and the king went along with this plan.

What should Esther do? Not only to save herself but all the Jewish people? At Mordecai's encouragement—made famous by his exhortation, "Who knows whether you have not come to the kingdom for such a time as this?"—Esther got up the courage to confront the king and admit his decree would mean killing his new queen too. She interceded for her people and asked the king to spare their lives.

And it worked! Esther's action saved a whole generation of Jewish people—which is important for even us today because Jesus our Savior came from the lineage of Abraham and was Jewish. Esther's courage to speak up kept God's plan in motion.

Here's what I want you to see in the story of Esther. She used her voice to speak into a situation that was right in front of her. *Her voice mattered.* She used it to make a difference, to stand up for what was right. And although approaching the king with that request was likely the most difficult thing she'd ever done, God had equipped her for the task. The voice she used was the voice she already had . . . whether she knew she had it in her or not.

————

It's not just Esther though. I'm reading through the entire Bible this year in chronological order—my first time to ever attempt it. When I get to the end of this year and can say I read the entire Bible from cover to cover in the past year, it might be one of the top accomplishments of my lifetime. (Again with the drama, Jamie? Come on.)

Around March of my reading, we were in the book of Numbers—sort of an unlikely place, you'd think, for having a moment in God's Word where you really want to lean in close. But it was a story where God honored five women who used their voices boldly and confidently before their leader Moses and ultimately before God.

Numbers 26 is basically a census update. The people of Israel were nearing the Promised Land, and this population

report would determine how the land was to be divvied up
once they moved in and occupied it. Then, Numbers 27.
The accounting was over, and five daughters of a deceased
man named Zelophehad stood before Moses and pleaded
their case. Their father had died without bearing any sons.
And under traditional rules of that time, daughters did not
inherit land from their fathers. Only sons did. If there were
no sons, then brothers. And if no brothers, then on to the
nearest male relative.

The girls were going to be left out. And if they were given
no land as their father's inheritance, his name would eventually be forgotten. So they stood up for themselves, as well as
for the memory of their father, asking for land they thought
they deserved.

I think of the courage and persistence it must have taken
for these ladies to work their way up through the leadership
structure, making their appeal to whoever would hear them.
Moses, you see, wouldn't have been their first stop. Tiers of
judges were in place to handle people's problems. Only if
none of them could settle the issue would it get bumped up
to Moses.

But these women, after taking their request to the judges,
finally did appear before Moses, who then took it before God.
The Lord instructed him to give these women the land their
father was to inherit, then took it a step further by declaring
a new law in regards to how daughters were treated in matters
of land delegation.

And if I were still having babies, I would pick one of these ladies and name my daughter after her. (Maybe not Hoglah . . . maybe Tirzah.) I would then tell the story of that woman's courage and strength to my daughter before tucking her into bed each night! These women had no platform, no position. They were just regular women like you and me. Yet they used their voice to address what was right in front of them. And God took notice. He used them to advance His own purposes.

———

Four months into my radio career, I was certain I'd found my new career path. I enjoyed my coworkers. The voice I discovered was fulfilling something in me that I never knew was missing. For the first time in a long time, I felt as though my life was mattering for something, that God had put this job in my life so He could use my gifts in a new and fresh way.

But even as my work life was thriving, my home life was falling apart. My kids were struggling with Mom now working every day outside of the home. My marriage was struggling with my new work hours and how tired they left me. I was in love with my life from the hours of 6:00 to noon. But every other hour in the day felt like it wasn't grooving with my newfound love.

I knew I needed to make a change. And the change was me quitting the job I'd grown to love so much. I sat down with Aaron one day and expressed my concern over our family, feeling like everything was falling apart at home. It wasn't like he hadn't noticed; I mean he lived there as well!

I quit my new career, four months in.

I quit the career that made me feel as though I'd found my dream job.

I quit the career that I felt had given me a voice for the first time in my life.

It was the best and hardest decision I'd ever made. And to be honest, I was a little angry about it. I felt angry that God had opened doors and put me in a position to win this job, only to make me choose between my kids or my career. I was even a little frustrated that Aaron wasn't having to make this same kind of choice. (Not proud about feeling this way either.) He was thriving in his career, yet I was the one who had to leave mine to stay home with the kids.

I was throwing the biggest pity party you've ever seen, and Aaron patiently let me have my moment. He knew how much I loved this new job and how hard this decision was. Little did I know, however—and this is the part we always need to leave room for in the midst of our questions and disappointments—God was doing something way bigger in my life than I could see at the time.

I said often after quitting my job that the thing I missed most from my radio days was not having a voice anymore. The ability to influence people with my words felt new to me, and I believed I'd discovered a gift for using my words to show people Jesus.

But as with the story of Queen Esther, as with the daughters of Zelophehad, my radio journey showed me that the voice you and I have been given to point others to Jesus, or to stand up for what's right, even to petition our requests to the Father, has been inside us from the get-go. Esther wasn't given her voice only when she decided to defend her people against injustice. The daughters of Zelophehad didn't wake up one day with a voice that had never been theirs before. No, they each had their voice all along. And God used it for so much good.

I know and believe now, 100 percent, my voice was mattering long before I piped it through a microphone at that radio station.

You have a voice too, and you can use it for big things, right where you are.

So after I'd worked through my disappointment with giving up something important to me—giving it up for the fabulous job of being present with my kids—I began to think more about using my voice for good where God had planted me. I realized after the fact that my voice hadn't gotten bigger or stronger or more valuable just because I'd been working in radio. My

You have a voice too, and you can use it for big things, right where you are.

voice—and your voice too, my friend—contains power wherever we choose to use it. That's where it's the loudest and most effective, when you direct it toward those people who are right in front of you.

This could mean your children, your Sunday school class, the PTA meetings, a stage, your parents, your coworkers, your employees, your neighbors. Wherever God has placed you is where your voice works best.

I'm thankful that God has placed me in a season today where I can use my voice through my podcast, my books, through speaking at events. Doesn't make me any more special than anyone else; it's just where God has put me—that's all that mat-

> **Wherever God has placed you is where your voice works best.**

ters—and I'd be unfaithful not to work hard for Him there. But I'm even more humbled and honored that God has seen fit to place me in a home with children who need my voice more than anyone else needs it. I have a son who right now is closer to graduating from high school than I'd like to think, and my voice in his life is one of the most cherished gifts that God has ever given me.

Trust Him with where He has you. Your voice has power. You can use your voice for the glory of God wherever you are.

For me, it took discovering the voice I didn't know I already had, then thinking I'd lost that voice forever, before I finally realized I had that voice inside me all along. God just uses it differently in different stages of our lives. It doesn't show up when something "big" arrives. Your voice is already there, and your job is to steward it well toward whoever is right in front of you listening.

You can use your voice for the glory of God wherever you are.

No voices are better than others; they're just different. Your voice never changes; it just reaches those best who are in front of you at the moment.

My friend LaTasha Morrison is such a good example of using her voice to speak into what's right in front of her. You might know her name now, but before Tasha started Be the Bridge,[8] or stood on massive stages, or got invited to do things with Facebook, she was saying the same things to a group of women in Austin that no one knew about.

---

[8] Be the Bridge is an organization that equips people to deal authentically and redemptively with the injustices of racial division. Find out more at https://bethebridge.com/.

Tasha once invited a group of us to meet at the African-American Cultural and Heritage facility to talk about race and unity. I honestly had no idea what I was walking into that day. I did know these conversations were important to me because three of my children look different than me. I also knew these conversations should matter to all of us as Christians. But I was not prepared for what meeting with these ladies would do for my soul and my heart over the next few years.

Tasha led us so well. She guided our conversations about race, unity, privilege, and so much more. The group was diverse, and God used the voices that were represented in that room to shape me and continue bringing value into my life today. Tasha wasn't writing books then; she wasn't on a large stage. She was ministering to the children in her church as the kids' director and using the voice God had given her from the day she was born, using it to move the hearts of those around her. She was using her voice to teach, lift up, and encourage the ones that God had put in front of her at that specific moment.

This was the beginning of Tasha's now "big" voice she uses through her organization. But it sounded just as big to me those years ago when her stage was a lot smaller. She didn't wait for the platform to get bigger before she cranked up the volume on what God had given her to say.

Don't wait to be invited to a larger table before you sit down and share what's inside you. You and your voice are already invited to the table. And there, you get to use your voice to bring change to the world. You get to use your voice to spread the gospel. You get to use your voice to make Him known and bring Him glory. You get to use your voice not because you've earned it or deserve it or because you're the best person for the job, but simply because God has invited you into this work with Him. He places value on you and adores you as His daughter. No further invitation is needed. Your invite is the love of God in you, using you to speak to the people right in front of you.

Don't wait to be invited to a larger table before you sit down and share what's inside you.

Your words matter. Your ideas have value. Now go use them. Steward those words, ideas, and thoughts well. Look around you, see who's in front of you, and speak to them. Speak with boldness, confidence, love, and grace that comes from the Father, and tell them the good news.

- Your kids need to hear your voice.
- Your parents need to hear your voice.
- Your spouse needs to hear your voice.
- Your neighbors need to hear your voice.
- Your children's teachers, your friends at the gym . . .

- Your coworkers, your roommate, other students down the hall . . .
- Your classmate in biology, your cousins across the country . . .
- Your Bible study ladies, your followers on social media . . .
- The other side of the world needs to hear your voice.

God gave it to you. Own it. And go use it!

Chapter 4

Simple Math

Maximizing Your Gifts

I'm about to tell you something that could easily push me down a few notches on your "good Christian" scale, which—let's be honest—if you've got one of those scales, we need to have a different conversation about why you have a good Christian scale in the first place.

So let me rephrase. I'm about to tell you something that might surprise you, knowing that my husband is a *pastor*. And here it is: When we travel, we don't go to church on Sundays.

There, I said it. How many notches did I just go down on that scale (the one you're not even supposed to have)? Hopefully none, because . . . again, hopefully you don't have a scale!

But it's true, this Sunday thing. If we're out of town on vacation with our family, or if it's just Aaron and I away and our trip overlaps a Sunday, we're sleeping in and going to brunch somewhere.

My husband did not grow up like that. He's a PK (preacher's kid) and his family was super religious. If they were out of town on a Sunday, here's what *they* would do. They would find the local church affiliated with their denomination, and they would go there for Sunday worship. When they did, I'm most confident the pastor would ask, "Do we have any visitors today?" and my husband and his family would wave their hands to acknowledge being in from out of town. I'm also confident they probably had to stand up and say what town they were from and all that jazz.

I would hate that so much. If you're a churchgoing person now and you've never been to a church where they do the whole meet-and-greet thing during the service, just know I hate it as much as you do. And I'm a pastor's wife. I'll never like it. Ever.

Forget I said that. Let's just get back to where I was going with this whole story.

There actually has been *one* time in our marriage that we were out of town together when a Sunday rolled around and we did go visit another church. It was February 4, 2018, and the reason I remember that date is because I was on my very first book tour for my very first book. But on that Sunday—at Passion City Church in Atlanta—I heard Louie

Giglio preach one of those messages that just forever stuck with me. He titled it "Boost or Bury," and I've never been the same since hearing it.[9] Do you know what I mean? You have those messages too, right? You remember where you were sitting; you remember what you were feeling; you might even remember what you were wearing. Life-changing messages about the gospel can just *stick* with you like that.

I'll never forget, for example, a sermon that Halim Suh preached at our church one time about Mary anointing Jesus' feet at Bethany in the days before He was crucified. I'll never forget Christine Caine preaching at Passion 2020 about filling up our dry wells with the living water of Jesus. I'll never forget David Platt preaching so clearly about following Jesus that I thought I needed to get saved again.[10] Or the time I heard Jen Wilken preach on Rahab, and how the tears just streamed down my face.

This was one of those kinds of messages for me. It apparently fell in the middle of a sermon series they were doing called "Journeying around the Sun," about the trip our planet makes around the sun each year, and how we need to make the current year of our life really count. Messages like these really fire me up, which is probably why that day stands out to me so much, and also probably why I'm writing this book!

---

[9] You can hear it (watch it) yourself at passioncitychurch.com/gathering/boost-or-bury/.

[10] Obviously you never need to get saved again.

Louie's message that Sunday was from Matthew 25 on the parable of the talents.

Before we jump in and I give you my take on this passage, let me remind you of the definition of a parable. A parable is a simple story used to illustrate a moral or spiritual lesson. Jesus used parables many times in His teaching to communicate a particular lesson or principle He wanted to convey. Parables are just stories with a meaning.

And here, I think, is one of the first things this parable means.

You Already Have Enough Talent

> "For it will be like a man going on a journey, who called his servants and entrusted to them his property. To one he gave five talents, to another two, to another one, to each according to his ability. Then he went away."

These "talents," in New Testament times, represented an amount of money. A *large* amount of money. I don't think it's a stretch, though, to say that Jesus' lesson here applies to more than just money alone. It incorporates all the things God has resourced us with—His gifts to us, His investments in our lives—things He's given to us that we can do something with. What we see in this story is a man giving his

servants access to his property by distributing to them a dif-
fering amount of talents, "to each according to his ability."

This is the part we can't miss—the "each according to
his ability" part—or else it begins to seem unfair that one of
them received five talents, another two, and the last servant
received only one. This parable has nothing to do with the
actual number of talents these people received; what matters is what they *did* with their talents. They received talents
according to their ability. They received the amount that was
the best fit for them, as decided by their master and not by
their own wishes and desires.

One thing I see happening these days is people struggling with the talents and gifts they've been given. They don't
appreciate their talents, or they wish they had other talents,
talents that seem *better* in their eyes.

The world does a really good job of adjusting the value
of our talents. But this parable is meant to tell us how the
kingdom of God works, as opposed to how the world works.
And in this story, like in the kingdom, each person received
the right amount of talents for themselves and for the ful-
fillment of their purpose. They received exactly what they
needed from their master. He wasn't holding out on them.
He wasn't playing favorites. He was handing out what each
one needed, based on their ability.

I've had more conversations than I'd like to admit with
women who wish they had different gifts and talents than
they do. It's not even that I think they want *different* talents;

they just think other people's talents are better, and they want in on that. We're going to dive into this topic later when we talk more specifically about contentment, but for now it's enough to recognize that God has equipped you and me with exactly what we need for doing the work He wants us doing on this earth.

Let's go way back to the beginning of your life. No matter how you showed up, whether you were born into a mom-and-dad family that was overflowing with love, or you were placed for adoption after your birth, or your home seemed more like a war zone than a place where a family would thrive, know that God crafted you in your mother's womb. He took great pleasure in creating you to be you! With *your* talents. Exactly as He wanted.

When I look back on my life and think about the talents I've had since elementary school, and how God is using them in me now and developing them in ways that help me tell others about Jesus, I'm blown away at the masterful plan He had for my life. He truly equips us to do His good works, just like we're supposed to, just like He says He will.

Forgive me for using a sports analogy, if that's not what you were expecting from me, but I'm a girl who loves sports. I have three boys who all play football. And on the one hand, of course, I love it. I love the game. I love going to their games. We have season tickets to the University of Texas games, so I love watching football—on TV, in person, wherever. I love it all. We do live in Texas, and football in Texas is life!

Except for the idea that my boys could get hurt.

We held off on football as long as we could, because in Texas it's no biggie for first-grade boys to load up in full gear, pads, and helmets, and play tackle football. It's true that watching first graders trying to tackle each other is pretty cute, since most of them can barely move in all that football gear. But we decided to wait until sixth grade before we let our kids play. We felt like we were somehow making better choices about their ability to keep from getting hurt.

All three of my boys play different positions because their different skills are what make them valuable to their teams. One of my boys, for instance, hasn't hit a big growth spurt yet. He's smaller than other kids his age. A lot of the middle school girls, in fact, are taller than him, and I think I could throw him soaking wet across the room with one hand. So he will clearly not be playing on the offensive or defensive line this next season. He doesn't have what it takes for that position. Playing on the line is not a *bad* thing; it's just not *his* thing. But he is super fast, and he is football smart, and his gifts and talents will do him well at playing *other* positions in a football game. He probably won't ever lead the team in sacks—he's not good at that—but he is good at doing what he's been given the body for.

I have struggled with this truth, with this concept, in my career. I've had many moments of looking around at brilliant women who teach the Bible so well, and wondered if I should teach it more like them. I've looked around at women who write books and thought that maybe I should write more like them. I've often wondered if I have enough talent, because as I look around at other Bible teachers, I sure do see a lot of talent being represented.

I had a hard time at first accepting the talents that God had given me, mainly because they didn't look like the talents of other teachers I loved. We are fortunate to live in a day and age where women are getting more opportunities to teach the Bible, and now I can see what an honor it is to join the women that have been doing this faithfully for so many years.

As I said before, God has equipped each of us with exactly what we need for playing our part on His team. You already *have* your talent, and it is already enough. God wants me to be me, and He wants you to be you.

Your Talent Is Made to Be Used

> "He who had received the five talents went at once and traded with them, and he made five talents more. So also he who had the two talents made two talents more. But he who had received the one talent went and dug in the ground and hid his master's money."

We now get to the part where we see what the servants actually did with their talents while the master was away. And this is the part I get fired up about. Talking about what you *do* with your giftings gets me a tad bit excited.

Here's how it worked out in Jesus' parable: The first man took his talents, conducted business with them, and made five more talents. Doubled his investment. The second man took his talent and made two more talents. He, too, doubled his investment. The third servant, on the other hand, dug a hole in the ground and hid his talent. He did nothing productive with it.

And for just a couple of seconds, I want to talk real straight with you. If digging holes to hide your talent is something you're in the habit of doing, I might just need to give you a little kick in the pants, because you haven't been doing anything with the talents God has given you. Remember, this parable has nothing to do with the *number* of talents these people had, but everything to do with what the person *did* with his talents after the master left town.

Why do you think you've been burying your talent?

Maybe you've been burying it because you think it's not as good as someone else's. You look around and compare yourself to others, and think you shouldn't do anything with your talent because it's so seemingly small.

Or maybe you bury your talent because you've been burned by trying to use your gifts and talents before, and you don't want to feel that feeling ever again. You tried once and it didn't go too well, so instead of trying again, you've decided to bury what God has given you out of fear of rejection, fear of the unknown, or fear of failure.

But here's how you put a stop to that faulty logic. In order to be the kind of servant who puts yourself out there to double your talent, like the wise servants in Jesus' story, you need to be willing to say, "This isn't about *me*; this is about me using what God has given me to bring Him glory."

I just want to burst your bubble for a moment, if you don't mind. *Your talents were never meant for you.* They were given to you by the God of the universe so that you could serve others. As Peter the apostle said, writing in Scripture, "Each of you should use whatever gift you have received to serve others, as faithful stewards of God's grace in its various forms." The secret to being more faithful in using your talents is by turning your focus away from how they reflect on *you* and more onto how God can put them to work in helping the people around you.

When you think about it this way, it'll take a bit of the fear out of your mind about using your gifts. It'll free you up from either (1) thinking you're Superwoman or (2) thinking you don't matter for anything.

The reason the two men doubled their talents wasn't because they were smarter businessmen than the third guy. The reason they were able to double their talents was simply because they *did* something with them. Look at what God has given you, and ask yourself how you're using your talents to serve others around you. If you can't come up with anything, you need to get your booty in gear and start doing something.

But let me tell you, even though I know I'm pushing you a little hard—I'm only doing it because of how hard I've had to push myself as well. This passage just messes me up. I don't want to be a burier, though sometimes burying my talents has seemed way easier than stepping out of my comfort zone.

I'll never forget the day, for instance, when I almost quit my ministry before it had barely started. I was at a conference in South Carolina where I was scheduled to lead a breakout session on podcasting. I'd only been a podcaster for about fifteen months, but I guess they figured I knew what I was doing. Or maybe everyone else they asked was busy! This was the second biggest thing I'd ever spoken at, and it was one of my first few times to fly to an event where I was speaking. Everything was so new to me. I felt way out of my league.

While checking into my hotel for the event, people started coming up to talk with me. I was getting recognized for the first time, and honestly it was amazing to meet listeners of my show.[11] That's the thing with the work that I do. I do all of it mostly alone, so to meet actual humans who listen to my voice is so much fun.

---

[11] Also, please note: if we ever meet and you tell me you listen to my show or have read one of my books, I will automatically hug you. Or elbow-bump you. Or not hug you but pretend like I'm hugging you. Whatever we're doing these days to show affection at a safe distance. Sorry if that's not your thing. I'm just grateful for you, that's all.

But these weren't the only "firsts" happening for me that weekend. I had meetings with two potential literary agents, as well as with representatives from a number of publishing houses. I was like the little schoolgirl on her first day of kindergarten hanging out with all the fifth graders. I knew *nothing*, and yet I was having meetings and conversations about big things—big career things that I'd imagined but never really thought would be a reality for me.

At one point in the day, however, after a meeting with a third editor, I nearly had a breakdown right there in the hotel lobby.

Almost instantly I felt overwhelmed by this need to run away, to get alone in my room as quickly as possible. It was just an onslaught of fear and apprehension. I thought people were being fooled by me. I imagined failing everyone who thought they wanted to partner with me. And I needed to get away from it. I wasn't up for this.

The tears had already started overflowing from my eyes when I rounded a corner, mere feet from my room, and ran into Sarah—a woman I'd never met but who I'd loved and adored from afar. I don't know what I must have looked like, but my desperation was apparently noticeable enough that she stopped me and asked if I was okay, and I word-vomited all my feelings of inadequacy and fear. Right there in the hallway. We had never met before! And I just unloaded my guts on her!

But even though she was nothing less than kind, and offered me great wisdom assuring me that I would indeed survive, I left there and got into my room as fast as I could, put on my pajamas, and climbed into bed . . . because the obvious way to deal with this feeling was to put myself to bed! This may or may not be a default of mine when life feels hard, to just go back to bed!

I snuggled under the covers and prepared not to leave from there until my session time came up, after which I determined I would come back and resume this same prone position until it was time to get on my flight. I would not, *could* not, have any more conversations with anyone.

Except my husband. I called to tell him about my plan for hotel-room lockdown. And without even hesitating, he told me to get myself together, get dressed, and get back downstairs. (Sort of like how I was talking to you earlier!) That's because he knew something I couldn't quite understand. I had gifts and talents that God was about to use in a new way. And, yes, it would make me uncomfortable in the process. But remember, he said, I wasn't going to be using these gifts for *me;* I was going to be using them to serve God and to serve those around me, which Aaron knew was my real desire in the deepest places of my heart.

I laugh every time I remember the internal crisis I experienced at that conference. I was so unbelievably scared. And my fears seemed so justified. I didn't think I was even all that good at the job I was currently doing, and now people were wanting to meet with me and partner with me because they believed in me and my work. Seriously? My mind and my heart were so confused. I just wasn't sure I was cut out for this job.

Let me ask: What is it for you? What are you holding onto so tightly because you feel inadequate? What gifts are you hoarding because you aren't confident anyone will want them? What keeps you from taking your talent and multiplying it? A lot of it for me was fear.

But my fears didn't die down when I left South Carolina. After I'd signed a book deal, even after I'd started working on the writing, I remember pulling my friend Annie aside at church one day and confessing that I didn't think I could do this public ministry thing. I confessed to her my fear that pride could be the downfall of me, that fame would take me out in a heartbeat if I succumbed to it.

I told her that I was seriously thinking of foregoing this book project and the whole idea of being an author and speaker. I just wasn't sure it was *for* me. My fear of the unknown and the sin struggles in my own life were causing me to think about letting the whole opportunity go, just bowing out. God was bringing my talents to the surface and I was scared of them. Success seemed to be on the horizon, but I didn't think I could handle it. I was convinced that what I thought to be success would take me under.

I think in that moment, those words I was saying sounded super-spiritual to me—you know, that I was being self-aware enough to realize how so-called success would capture my heart and become an idol to me, and how I was going to do whatever I needed to do, at whatever sacrifice to my personal ambitions, to prevent anything from becoming more important to me than the Lord. So I would just bury it. I would sit on it. I wouldn't do anything. I was taking my talent and hoarding it. For everyone's good. How enlightened of me.

Annie paused for a silent moment before looking back at me and confidently saying, "Do you think everyone who's been given a gift for writing, speaking, or podcasting is immune to those struggles?"

I thought about it for a second, then gave her the obvious answer: "No. I'm sure they struggle with those as well."

"You've been given a gift, Jamie," she kindly rebuked me. "And what you need to do is *fight your sin,* not throw away your gifting."

Mic drop.

Your Talent Is Meant to Be Multiplied

> "Now after a long time the master of those servants came and settled accounts with them. And he who had received the five talents came forward, bringing five talents more, saying, 'Master, you delivered to me five talents; here I have made five talents more.' His master said to him, 'Well done, good and

faithful servant. You have been faithful over a little; I will set you over much. Enter into the joy of your master.'

"And he also who had the two talents came forward, saying, 'Master, you delivered to me two talents; here, I have made two talents more.' His master said to him, 'Well done, good and faithful servant. You have been faithful over a little; I will set you over much. Enter into the joy of your master.'"

The master arrived back home, prepared to receive an account from his three servants, and the first two approached to let him know what they'd done with what he'd left them. I'm not saying they came to him boasting, but I'd like to think they were proud of their work. Almost like, "Look what I did with what you gave me!"

I so want that person to be me. And I so want that person to be you. I want us to show up at the end of our lives, eager to say, "Look, Lord—look at what I did with what You gave me!" We took it, we used it, we invested it, we served with it.

We *multiplied* it.

Notice again that the two people in this portion of the parable began with different amounts of talents, yet they received the same proclamation of approval from the master. The one with five talents who doubled his investment received the same reward as the one who started with two talents and doubled his as well.

I've said it and I'll say it again: *It's not about how much talent you have; it's what you do with what's been given to you.*

My friend Annie (yes, the same Annie from earlier) immediately comes to mind when I think about someone multiplying her talents. She has volunteered in every department at our church throughout her time of being there. She's volunteered in production; she's written curriculum; she's led teams of writers. I wouldn't be surprised if she's even served in the nursery at one time or another. She's married to Kyle, who works with my husband, and they have two of the cutest kids around.

Here's what I've seen in Annie's life over the past few years that always causes me to pause and thank God for her. She's been given the gift of writing and communicating. It's a proven gift, and she has stewarded it well. Prior to having kids, she wrote many of the in-house Bible studies that our church has gone through, and she is highly trusted by our pastors and elders in what she writes.

Then enter babies. If you've ever had kids, or been around kids, or even *seen* a kid, you know they are all-consuming. They never stop moving, talking, grooving, walking, until they crash into bed at whatever time they finally go to sleep. Taking care of kids is a full-time job, and Annie has had to figure out ways to still use her gifts of writing and teaching while also being a momma to her babies.

I know this can be a tricky conversation. You may already feel your defenses rising up. But I want to challenge you just a bit (if you're a parent) to think about how you can love your babies with all your heart *while* using your gifts to serve others around you and point them to the Lord.

Annie has worked tirelessly at this, and it hasn't always been easy. She's hired babysitters; she's worked late-night hours; she's worked early-morning hours before any of us desire to be awake; she's given up some of her other responsibilities, as well as some of her other pleasures. Annie has taken the gifts that God has given her, and instead of succumbing to the idea that this time in her life apparently can't be a season for using her writing gifts, she's adjusted and found unique ways to still serve Him in her writing.

Now don't get me wrong. It looks different than pre-kids. The amount of time she spends writing is considerably less and more compact than before becoming a momma.

But God didn't somehow forget that Annie was a great writer when he gifted her with her children. And I believe He delights in the way she is multiplying her talents day-by-day because of her faithfulness to Him.

God knew your talents, your gifts, and the role you would play in this world when He blessed you with kids. But I meet a lot of women who enter motherhood and completely give up serving those around them or living out their gifts, talents, and passions. It saddens me deeply to see that. I truly believe you can be a phenomenal momma *and* use your giftings for the church.

It just takes a little math. And a lot of hard work. But pretty soon, you've learned to multiply.

Your Talent Gains Nothing by Hoarding

> "He also who had received the one talent came forward, saying, 'Master, I knew you to be a hard man, reaping where you did not sow, and gathering where you scattered no seed, so I was afraid, and I went and hid your talent in the ground. Here, you have what is yours.' But his master answered him, 'You wicked and slothful servant! You knew that I reap where I have not sown and gather where I scattered no seed? Then you ought to have invested my money with the bankers, and at my coming I should have received what was my own with interest.'"

Doesn't end up looking too good for this last guy, does it? He came before the master explaining why he didn't do one single thing with his talent. And from the sound of his response, he sincerely thought he was doing what was best. He at least had a long explanation.

And I get it. Don't you? He didn't necessarily do anything bad; he just didn't do *anything*. Sometimes when I come home from work during the summer and my kids are lying around letting their brains turn into mush from TV and video games, I'm frustrated with them—not because they did anything wrong, but because they didn't do anything at all!

Laziness can obviously be a big part of our problem in this area. As can the stagnation that sets in when we refuse to grow and multiply because we don't have what others have. I'm always pained seeing people who want more influence, more gifts, more talents, more fill-in-the-blank, when they're not being faithful with what God has put in front of them right where they are.

Women will say to me, "I want to write a Bible study; how do I contact someone about publishing it?" and my immediate response to them is: "Where are you teaching now?" You'd be surprised how many of them tell me they aren't teaching anywhere. I guess they only want to teach on big stages and distribute their studies through a publishing company. They're not using their gifts in the places where God has put them because they're constantly wanting more.

But the underlying culprit behind hoarding our talents is always fear. Listen to the man admit it in this parable: "I was afraid, and I went and hid your talent in the ground." Fear led him not to do anything with the talent his master had invested in him. The same fear that can drive us to do crazy things in life can also drive us to do *nothing* with our lives

You get one chance—*one chance*—to make a difference right where you are. You don't need to travel to the ends of the world to make a difference (although if that's what God asks of you, please go), but use your talents to serve those around you. Don't do *nothing* with them just because you're afraid.

You have talents. You have gifts. You have people in front of you who need serving and pointing to Jesus. So go do it! Don't wait for more gifts, for "bigger" gifts. Use what God gave you, and you will hear from Him what He said in verse 21: "Well done, good and faithful servant. You have been faithful over a little; I will set you over much. Enter into the joy of your master."

You Don't Want to Go Where Fear Will Take You

> "'So take the talent from him and give it to
> him who has the ten talents. For to every-
> one who has will more be given, and he will
> have an abundance. But from the one who
> has not, even what he has will be taken away.
> And cast the worthless servant into the outer
> darkness. In that place, there will be weeping
> and gnashing of teeth.'"

I don't mean to be dramatic here. (Aww, of course I do.) But this master is ticked.

I'm sorry, did he just say to "cast the **worthless**[12] servant into the outer darkness"? Yes, I believe he did. He is not playing around with this man who did NOTHING with his talent. This servant had the same opportunity to multiply his gifts as the men before him. But out of fear, which turned into laziness, which turned into bad stewardship, he chose to bury his talent.

This is the part of the passage that should rattle us a little bit. We should take it seriously when we hear Jesus speak of how frustrated this man became with his servant. Because if we put all the characters in place from this parable Jesus told, the master is our heavenly Father, and these servants are you and me.

And if we do nothing with the talents we've been given, God is not happy about that. Hard to paint a smiley face on "cast the worthless servant into the outer darkness," don't you think?

But yet this parable isn't meant to scare the heck out of us. As with everything the gospel means, it's meant to spur us into returning and repenting so that He can free us up to serve Him and serve others, to do great and mighty things for the kingdom of God.

---

[12] The **boldness** of that word is all mine!

In thinking how you're likely to feel after reading this chapter, I imagine you as being one of three types of people:

- You're someone who is chasing hard after God, who is using your gifts and talents not for your own good but to serve others and make Him known.[13]
- You're someone who is serving but is constantly looking around and comparing yourself to the gifts and talents of others around you. You're wondering how to get more opportunities to serve. You're wondering how to have a bigger impact. You're wondering why your talents are X and hers are Y, Y, Y. Her talents seem a whole lot better.[14]
- You're someone who is scared and doing nothing. God has prompted you to serve, give, and step out of your comfort zone, but you've refused. Or you have talent for days, yet you're using almost all of it to build up yourself.[15]

---

[13] Yes, you are amazing, but please don't get cocky.
[14] Don't feel bad. We've all been there.
[15] We've all been here too, but please don't stay there.

This parable of the talents speaks to all of us—a warning to be diligent and unafraid, an encouragement to thrive and multiply.

> "For to everyone who has will more be given,
> and he will have an abundance."

However small you might feel your talents to be, they are part of the journey to your abundant life. Now go and multiply!

Part II

Accepting Yourself

Chapter 5

Going Green

The Trouble with Comparison

You've heard the old phrase: "The grass is greener on the other side." But is it more than just a phrase to you? Have you bought into it? Into the *lie* of it?

Because that's what it almost always is. The "grass is greener" proverb is rarely if ever reflective of the truth. And yet every one of us at one time or another has found ourselves believing it, or at least being susceptible to it. We've looked around at other situations, at our friends and other people, perhaps even total strangers, and wondered how much better our lives would be if we had what *they* had.

We do it by second nature, almost by involuntary reflex—this looking around and wondering why everyone has it so much better. We do it in almost every aspect of our lives.

- *At work:* when someone gets a promotion that we're convinced we deserve.
- *In our parenting:* when someone else's kids seem easier to deal with than ours.
- *All the time:* just in passing, sizing up other people's personality traits, their charisma, their physical appearance, their seamless lack of effort in social skills.

Have you ever wished for someone else's life? Or should I say, someone else's "green grass"? Not just, "Oh, I sure would like to have the (whatever) that she has." More like, "The life God has given me is not good, but if I had a life like hers, not only could I be happy, but I could be more useful. I could be a better person."

Ouch. I've been there more times than I'd like to admit.

Sometimes it shows up as jealousy or envy or greed, but at the root of all these problems is a lack of trust in what God has given us and where He's put us. We want more. We want different. We are *insecure* about who God has made us to be. As author Richella J. Parham says, "Insecurity is both the root of comparison and the fruit of comparison."

Here's another quote of hers that I like from *Mythical Me: Finding Freedom from Constant Comparison*: "Whatever aspect of ourselves we might be measuring, comparing ourselves to others usually leads to one of two results: (1) we feel *less than*, which can lead to shame, self-pity, ingratitude, jealousy, or envy of others; or (2) we feel *greater than*, which can lead to self-righteousness, arrogance, or disdain for others."

I've seen both of these gross comparison methods in myself throughout my life, as far back as third grade, when I would watch people open presents and think I deserved as much as they did, if not more. But I think we'd all agree the emergence of social media has made the comparison trap almost inescapable today. At any moment in time, we can see what anyone else is doing based on what they choose to show us. We look at their photos and compare them to the pictures of ourselves that we carry around in our own minds. *Their* photos show us their best (which is somewhere short of the real truth), while *ours* capture what goes for reality. If not worse.

Comparison is just everywhere.

Even when we're not looking for it.

I can tell you of a time, for instance, when someone almost *forced* comparison on me, and how it created a much bigger battle in my head than should have been there.

It happened at the gym. Where else?

If you take a typical mom who visits her local gym a few times a week, she's there for only a few reasons. And none of them have to do with her actual workout plans. Now of course there are exceptions to this rule. I have a few friends who do go to the gym for no other reason than to work out, but most of my friends make their regular visits to the gym a priority only because it offers them what?

Alone time.

Yes, and you know it's true. The gym is often the only spot in the day when a mom can ever be alone. I remember reading Angie Smith's book *I Will Carry You* while walking on a treadmill at my local YMCA. Do you know how slowly you need to be walking in order to read a book at the same time? *V-e-r-y* slowly. Do you know how slowly you need to be walking in order to sob while reading said book and walking on the treadmill? Even s-l-o-w-e-r.

I would get to the gym on the days I could go and would check my kids into childcare, then start my two-hour count-down window. Because that's how long they would watch them for free. Then I'd piddle around the gym for, oh, about an hour. I'd read (I mean, walk) on the treadmill—you know, to get that heart rate going. Then I might do a bit of rowing, but not too much because rowing while reading is *so* difficult, let me tell you. Then I'd head into one of the workout classes, not to join the workout, just to stretch (and read at the same time). That I can do. Then I'd go lift a few weights before it was time to hit the showers.

Because if being alone is our chief motivation for frequenting the gym, the number-one part of that alone time is being able to shower and get ready. Alone. I really looked forward to that.

One particular day, though, after I'd worked out (and probably read a whole book!) and was toweling off after my shower, a woman approached me and started talking to me. Now I don't mind talking to people at the gym, and I don't even mind talking to people in the locker room, but I do mind talking to people while I'm getting dressed after showering.

Yet she continued to talk, and I continued to try politely ignoring her, even turning my back on her as I was getting dressed, until she asked the question of the hour: "How many kids do you have?"

Her question seemed innocent enough. It was at least an easy one to answer, even while I was hustling to change in front of her. I told her that I was a momma to four kids.

She gasped out loud. "Four kids?! You look amazing!" She then went on and on about how awesome my body looked after having "four kids! I can't believe it!" But as you know by reading this book, our family was formed by my birthing only ONE of those kids, after which we adopted three others.

So I could've corrected the confusion I'd accidentally created. I could've filled her in on our personal family history. But that would've taken even *more* time, would've led to even *more* questions, and . . . okay, I was kind of enjoying her praises. She was making me feel super good about how I looked, which is unlike how I typically feel when I stand in front of the mirror at home.

For all these reasons, I simply thanked her, without correcting her, and continued to get dressed. But if I thought the number-of-kids question was the question of the hour, the next one is what put this whole conversation over the edge.

She asked me how *old* my four children were.

Now here's where it's tricky. You see, two of my boys were born in the same year. Though they joined our family at different times, and though they're not biologically related, they are actually the same calendar age for about half of the year. And we were currently inside one of those overlapping time frames where they were both the same age.

So I rattled off the answer to her question: "eight, six, six, and four." And if I thought the sound of her first gasp was big, this second gasp topped them all. "And you had *twins?*" She almost fell off the bench where she was tying her shoes.

It was at this moment that I felt as though I couldn't go back. Would *you* have? I mean, she was so impressed with me, with the body that she believed had birthed four kids (including that set of twins, you know), and I was loving it. I wanted it to be true, even though it wasn't.

Yet I did have a choice. I could 'fess up right then and there and let her know that not only do I not have twins, but I only gave birth to one of my kids. I could have said that. But I didn't. Instead I just awkwardly nodded my head in a general *yes* motion and, avoiding further eye contact, quietly mouthed, "yep, even twins," realizing my body language couldn't keep up this charade much longer.

Goodbye, locker room person. I quickly got dressed and ran to the childcare facility to wrangle my precious babies, three of whom are black, before she found me and busted my whole four-kids-and-a-set-of-twins thing and made for *another* uncomfortable conversation.

I often go back to that story when I think of comparison because, although I wasn't the one doing the comparing in this case (because she was doing it all *for* me), it was just a back door into the same living space that I too often call home. It was no different than the times when I'd looked at *other* women's bodies and wondered why *they* had the figure I wanted. (It's probably because they weren't reading books on the treadmill!)

But whether less-than or greater-than, comparison is the perpetuation of a lie.

It is no way to nurture a *You Be You* lifestyle.

————

Why do we compare? What made that woman compare my body to what she thought the body of a woman who'd delivered four kids (including twins) should look like? What causes us to look at the "greener grass" and wonder how we can get our grass that green? What's in us that makes us want to appear and act like someone else?

Comparison on its own, you know, is not bad. When we're comparing which avocados to buy in the store, for instance, we look at two and pick the better one. When we're comparing houses to buy, we get the inspection reports and usually pick the one with the least amount of work needed. When we look at our spiritual journey, we can usually find and compare seasons of growth, spotting trends that help us learn from past experiences. When a student takes a test, the teacher compares the test answer to the correct answer to see if they're the same. That's how you get an accurate grade.

So comparison by itself is not bad. Comparison itself is not a sin. But what we're seeing today in our culture and in our hearts is a contagion of comparison that is leading us toward sinful actions, thoughts, and deeds, as well as toward harmful distortions of reality.

Lisa Bevere says:

> Comparison has a pull to it. If allowed to, it will always move you away from your truest center. Comparison will attempt to puff you up through the insidious vehicle of pride, or it will push you down through the tyranny of insecurity. Either way, it will not be long until you feel as though you are off-kilter and on the outside looking in.

Comparison can be healthy, yes, but watch out! Because it can also be a real danger.

Why? Because pride. Because envy. Because insecurity.

I'm going to share something with you that I've never said out loud to anyone besides my husband. It's embarrassing and humiliating, but it's the result of insecurity and a super ugly prideful heart. But if it'll help you in your battle with comparison, I'm willing to be honest enough to put it out here in print. (After all, it's just the two of us, right?)

If you're a creator of *anything*, you know that people can leave reviews on what you've created. If you own a restaurant, there are reviews galore on your service, your food, your environment, and anything else people want to review from their time eating with you. Authors all have reviews on their books. Podcasters have reviews on their shows. Artists have reviews on their art. Musicians have reviews on their albums. Photographers have reviews on their photography. People have opinions. And they're allowed to post them and share them and say anything they want about them.

Now on a particularly low day in my life, I gave in to a passing thought that suggested I should go read some of the bad reviews of my podcast on iTunes. Ask me why; I don't know. This isn't the first time I've done this, but every single time I do it, my husband questions my sanity. Because as Albert Einstein is famously reported as saying, "The definition of insanity is doing the same thing over and over again and expecting a different result." And he's right. I've never read bad reviews of myself or of my work and then walked away from that time feeling happy. I always feel sad and wonder if I should even keep doing what I'm doing. It usually ends with me concluding I should just quit and throw in the towel!

Well, on this day, after reading all of my bad reviews, I chose to navigate over to other podcasters' pages, reading the bad reviews of them and *their* shows too. And because I am very much a cheerleader of the people who work in my same media space of podcasting, especially of women podcasters, I know what I'm about to tell you is a good example of how strong and irresistible the pull of comparison can be on a person. If it could happen to me, it could happen to anybody.

Because instead of feeling sad for them also, the way I felt sad for myself—instead of being sympathetic and concerned for how their feelings might be hurt (although I hear most people have thicker skin than mine)—I began to feel a little boastful in the fact that some of their pages contained more one-star reviews than mine did. I found myself treasuring this time, relishing the few places where I seemed to be coming out ahead of them on the scorecard.

And all of a sudden, I began feeling better about myself than the way I'd felt only five minutes earlier. I found this comparison of our shows somehow enlivening. The hard evidence of black-and-white letters and numbers seemed to prove that I was indeed better than them.

How I cringe even as I write those words: *better than them.* It makes me sick. Comparison has a way of moving us toward the sin of pride. And as you probably know: of all the things God hates, maybe none of them is more disgusting than pride. "Everyone who is arrogant in heart is an abomination to the Lord," His Word says, "be assured, he will not go unpunished." I cringe when I write that word too: *abomination*.

But this prideful, "greater-than" form of comparison is typically a distant second to the kind that troubles most of us the most often: the kind of comparison that leaves us feeling "less-than," the kind that leads us into despair or grief over what we perceive someone else has that we don't have. That's the one we've found ourselves stuck inside so many times, over and over, ever since we were able to walk and talk as toddlers. Nothing new under the sun to describe here.

We do this in our parenting all the time. I remember being at Sea World[16] and noticing a family who seemed to be enjoying every single second while I was wondering how much longer my day could last. They had two girls around eight and ten who obeyed every word that came out of their parents' mouths, seemingly before the request had finished being uttered. They walked beside their parents. They drank their drinks without fighting, without counting the times their throats gulped and then demanding to get in one more gulp to make it even. My four kids, by contrast—ages seven, six, five, and three at the time—were running wild as if

---

[16] An amusement park that houses water animals. Think whales and seals. But not the whales that kill people anymore. They're apparently phasing out those shows slowly over time. Freeing one Willy at a time, I presume.

they'd never been allowed outside of their home before. They screamed for attention; one cried when a seal looked at her; and the others made me so anxious leaning over all the various aquarium railings that I was sure they would fall into the water and drown. (Again, rather dramatic, I know.)

I found myself imagining what my life would look like with two girls who held hands while skipping through the amusement park singing "Jesus Loves Me" to each other, as opposed to *my* four kids who were running around belting out "I Gotta Feeling" by the Black Eyed Peas.

Other times in my life I've looked at mothers who were able to leave the house each day for a job while I stayed home and changed diapers, made bottles, and watched what seemed like a never-ending lineup of *Dora the Explorer* and *Thomas the Train* each day. Other times in my life I've been jealous of women who had their master's degrees when all I had was a bachelor's. Other times in my life I've compared myself to the moms who volunteer for field trips all the time and have never missed a class party, while I often find myself working and unavailable. Recently I missed two of my oldest son's football games and immediately wondered if I was a bad mom, while comparing myself to my friend Tracy, who probably hasn't missed a game all year.

Envy is a terrible lie. It whispers to us that we deserve more and should get more. It leads us to wish that *our* life looked more like *her* life.

And it threatens to change the way we live—to change how we live our callings, change how we use our voice, change how we exercise our gifts and talents.

Comparison makes me want to hustle to be better than her. It makes me think if I'd just hustle more, I could beat what's making me feel so inferior to her. If I would do the five things she says she does, I'd be a better mom. I'd get the respect I see her getting that I think I deserve. I'd be more like the real person everyone thinks I am, if I would just do *that*—whatever "that" is. Comparison makes me think my success as a mom, friend, wife, or coworker is determined by how well I imitate her life. Because she sure makes it all look so easy.

Do you see the faultiness in this routine? Hustling for all the wrong reasons? Boasting in all the wrong things? Searching for all the wrong meanings and acknowledgments? Using the findings and feelings of comparison to dictate for us how we move toward satisfaction and success, rather than being directed by God's Word and staying true to our own calling?

It's a never-ending cycle that leads to more comparison, more pride, and always to more insecurity.

But what if we flipped this whole idea of comparison on its head? What if we took all the me-versus-she stuff completely out of the way? What if we became women who, instead of feeling the need to boast in ourselves, simply boasted in the One who made us who we are?

If we did, I have a small suspicion our lives would drastically change—in a way that moves us *toward* our callings, in a way that *opens up* our own voices, in a way that *maximizes* the abilities and sensitivities that God has created inside us. Instead of finding ourselves dissatisfied because of what we see in others, we would find ourselves truly satisfied in Him.

Paul the apostle said it best, I think, when he wrote, "Far be it from me to boast except in the cross of our Lord Jesus Christ, by which the world has been crucified to me, and I to the world."

He understood the damage that comparison could do. He wrote this verse to Christians in the ancient city of Galatia where the church had gotten caught up in a comparison controversy of its own. Influential but highly legalistic teachers were making demands on believers, insisting they needed to do certain things, perform certain rituals, and observe certain traditions, or else they weren't real Christians. And Paul was saying, *look*—if following all those steps was what it meant to be a success, his own upbringing made him almost perfect at it. People could've said, "Everybody look at Paul, compare yourself to Paul; everyone needs to be more like Paul." But Paul said not to look at *anybody* as a model now that Christ had come and shown us perfect living, perfect love, perfect truth, perfect grace. If you want to be proud of anything, he said, boast in what the cross of Jesus has done to heal your brokenness and to give you a reason for living.

On the *Journeywomen* podcast, Abigail Dodds said, "You can't obey God in someone else's life," and I couldn't agree more. God has asked us to live our *own* lives, not try imitating someone else's.

I'm not saying you can ever really curb the temptation of comparison altogether. It'll always be there. But like Paul said, we need to learn to be people who "take every thought captive to obey Christ." When you look at others, when you listen to them talk, when you feel the comparison impulse kicking in, force yourself to test it. Ask yourself: Who are these people pointing me toward? Are they pointing me toward themselves, or are they pointing me toward Christ?

Don't get hung up on whether they're a better parent, a better wife, a better teacher, a better whatever. Think instead: How could their example encourage me to chase hard after God's heart? Or, if you're sort of happy about their being in a *worse off* place than you happen to be—like I did with that podcaster—think instead: How could their current place of struggle encourage me to pray for them? How could their state of difficulty spark a heart of compassion in me, the kind of compassion Jesus has for me in my own moments of brokenness and struggle? Wouldn't I want someone praying for me that way if I was in their shoes?

That's how you use comparison for good. You let Him transform it into something that's actually able to help you grow. The reason you're looking at others now is to see how they're running hard after God and how you can learn from what they've learned by imitating Him themselves. Or, if they're doing terrible, you let it move you toward Christlike love and prayer.

"Be imitators of God, as beloved children." It all boils down to that. The only reason for using someone else's example as a guide for how you should live is found in how they help you imitate God, or maybe even pray to Him on their behalf. We'll never imitate Him perfectly, of course. But the good news is that because of Jesus we can strive for it, and be empowered by His Spirit in doing it, knowing that even when we fail and come up short, He has already given us His holiness to claim as our own.

Wonder why we're not satisfied by that?

───────

So as Paul said, "Set your minds on things that are above, not on things that are on earth." Think differently than those people whose sole focus is continually on comparing themselves with others or competing to become the kind of person this world is so enamored with, whether that person is you or not.

If you will commit to setting your mind "above" the normal places where you're tempted to do most of your comparing, the Bible says you will "therefore" begin putting to death "what is earthly in you: sexual immorality, impurity, passion, evil desire, and covetousness, which is idolatry"—all those things that stifle your freedom for living a faithful life.

And as those things slowly start to die off in you, you'll begin experiencing a revival of things like "compassionate hearts, kindness, humility, meekness, and patience, bearing with one another and, if one has a complaint against another, forgiving each other." Above all, Paul said, you'll find yourself able to "put on love, which binds everything together in perfect harmony."

Because when true love for others is in your heart, you can finally begin to implement what I've found to be one of the best ways of breaking free from the comparison trap of jealousy, pride, and envy.

Become a cheerleader for those around you.

It's harder to succumb to the sin of jealousy when you're actively trying to imitate God instead of giving in to your emotions. And it's hard to be jealous of someone when you are genuinely cheering them on. Notice I said *genuinely* because that's the only way this dynamic works out well, either for yourself or the person you're encouraging.

One of the highest compliments I've ever received came in the form of a text from my friend Tova, who said she saw my life as an example of living out the following quote by Bob Goff: "The more beauty we find in someone else's journey, the less we'll want to compare it to our own." How I hope I really do live up to that statement because it's one of my main goals in life. I so want to be a friend and cheerleader to those around me. I want it for a lot of reasons, but I'd be lying if I didn't say I'm motivated by one reason more than others. And here it is:

I want to be a cheerleader for others because
it's where unhealthy comparison goes to die.

I don't remember when this mind-set shifted in me, but I do know that being other people's biggest cheerleader has helped my heart put on the things that most imitate God.

Is it always easy? Obviously, no. It means when that other woman becomes pregnant for the fourth time, and you're on your second round of *in vitro*, you're still happy for her. You cheer for her. You're genuinely excited for her.

Does it mean you won't wrestle through emotions of sadness? Does it mean you'll never think, "Why isn't that happening for me?" No. But you can pray and talk about it with God. And when you do, He promises you "the peace of God, which surpasses all understanding"—peace that doesn't even make sense to you—that can "guard your hearts and your minds in Christ Jesus."

It means when your coworker is given the raise you wanted, or when someone else gets the clients you'd been working hard to develop, you can cheer on the other person and be thankful for the success they're enjoying. Although it's hard to celebrate their time in the spotlight while you may need to keep on working without the same recognition or benefit they're getting, God can give you the strength to do what you otherwise couldn't. Because the person who's walking in the Spirit can "look not only to his own interests, but also to the interests of others."

All because you've chosen the life and heart of a cheerleader.

Let's cheer for each other, not desire to *be* each other. Let's be thankful for their successes and not their failures. Let's keep our eyes on God as our ultimate example, as the One we most strive to look and be like, instead of focusing on someone we follow on social media, another mom at our church, the popular girl at school, or anyone else we think somehow has it better than us.

Comparison never looks good on you. But the smile of a cheerleader does. And the brightness of Jesus does. Don't let your thirst for being like somebody else steal another minute of your spiritual satisfaction. God will always give you what you need so that you can always be satisfied in who you're being and becoming.

> **Let's cheer for each other, not desire to *be* each other.**

Chapter 6

Selfie Satisfaction

The Struggle for Contentment

I remember the first time I felt real discontentment. I was only a teenager, but I wanted to be sixteen so badly I couldn't stand it. I couldn't wait to get my driver's license so that I could go places on my own and do whatever I wanted to do without asking, without being dependent on anyone else to take me.

But turning sixteen didn't solve my struggle with discontentment. Isn't it funny how each stage of life, as you make your approach to it, comes with all these ideas for what you think it will do for you, how you think it will be so much better for you, that it will finally provide you what you think you need for being perfectly content at last? I should've known from my experience with turning sixteen that not even graduating high school, or going off to college, or getting married, or having children would be the magic moment that made my whole life suddenly satisfying. Yet somehow we're always the first to be surprised when it isn't.

Because even though I was happy to get married—and *continue* to be happy in my marriage—it still didn't stop those feelings in me that thought the next thing in life would make me *really* happy. It then became: oh, I'd be so very happy with God and my life if I could just be a momma. Then if I could have *more* kids. Then if only I had a nicer house, a better car, a bigger diamond ring, a more satisfying job. The list just never ends. And I'm most confident you could write your own list in the margin, along with mine, of things you believed would finally make you happy if you could just achieve them. The list of what we think will make us happy never gets any smaller, not as long as our fleshly desires and ambitions are driving the satisfaction train.

Discontentment comes for us all, and it doesn't matter how old we are, what our marital status is, how many kids we have, how our career is going, what our appearance looks like, what kind of church we attend, or how much money we have or don't have. We all struggle with being content in our lives, wishing things were different.

When my youngest child was in prekindergarten, all I wanted was for her to get into all-day kindergarten. I dreamed of what my life would be like when all my kids were finally in school. I imagined all the freedoms I'd experience from 8:00 to 3:00 every weekday. I would finally be able to work on my podcast more, maybe schedule a haircut, or just lie around on the couch all morning if I wanted.

But the way I handled that year before my daughter went to school is high on the list of things I wish I could undo from my parenting journey. Because I wasted it. It was the last year I'd ever have with her all alone to myself. Instead I wished it away because I thought I'd be happier when it was over. I couldn't see the goodness God had given me in that moment I was currently living.

Thankfully His grace is so good to me when I think back on that time. He doesn't hold it over my head. But I would sure do it differently if I could go back. I would look at that year as a gift, not as something to endure and hope to hurry past.

I would relish being *content* inside it.

———

Now if we were to sit across the table from each other and I asked if you were content with where you are, with where God has taken you in life, you might first give me the Christian-ese answer. *Yes,* you'd tell me, knowing that's what we're all supposed to say. But if we had a way of peeking inside each other's hearts, of seeing what's truly inside there, I think we'd all be shocked at the level of discontentment many of us feel toward the lives we're currently living, even those of us who seem to have all the key components of blissful contentment. And I'm as sick of it as you are. Sick of it in me; sick of knowing it's probably in you too.

I do think social media plays the role of provocateur in all this. Discontentment was certainly in the world long before Instagram and Facebook, but we at least had places of retreat where, even if we'd *wanted* to know what was happening in other people's lives, we were limited by time and distance from actually seeing it with our own eyes.

In my grandparents' days, in my parents' days, even in my own early days of motherhood (which weren't *that* long ago, were they?) we all had little idea what others were really doing, enjoying, or experiencing. We knew generally what our friends were doing, but this information was mostly informed by whatever they told us when we were visiting together during our kids' playdates. We'd see our neighbors outside and go talk with them and ask about their families. Or when we'd get to work in the morning, we'd fill in our girlfriends about our date from the night before.

But there wasn't any neighborhood Facebook group where we trolled each other's posts. People didn't already know where we went to eat last night before they heard it from our own lips. The rhythm of life involved experiencing things, remembering things, and then sharing them face to face with others in person. The way we got to know each other was over dinner and through real human interaction, not by scanning their profile pages on LinkedIn.

But today at any moment, I can open up my phone, hit the Instagram button, and all of a sudden I'm seeing what all my friends are doing. I can see who got invited to speak at what conference I've never been invited to speak at. I can see which other pastor's wives dressed their children alike and had them to church on time with smiles on their faces. I can see what my other mom friends are packing in their kids' lunches (complete with super cute notes as well!) and I can see who's on vacation and what exotic dreamy location they've chosen. I can see the husband who brought flowers home to his wife on a random Wednesday, and what outfits my online friends are wearing on this ordinary day in their amazing lives, all while I look around my house at piles of laundry, unopened mail, dirty dishes, and random socks all over the floor.

For although we think these are examples of social media feeding us *information*, what it's really feeding us is *discontentment*. It's making us falsely believe that our life isn't good enough because it doesn't look like or measure up to the lives of people we follow online, or the people whose books we read, or the people we see on stage or TV—people who just seem to have the perfect everything.

We're walking around with this little device in our hands that can do so much good. I mean, I'm incredibly grateful for it. And yet at the same time, if you think about it another way, we're holding something dangerously close to our bodies that keeps causing us an enormous struggle with trusting God and being content with His plan for our lives.

And here's what's even crazier. While we're looking at others and determining their lives to be the standard, they're looking at us (and at others) and are coming to the same discontented conclusion. It's a vicious cycle that, if we aren't careful, can take us down.

Webster's definition of *discontentment* speaks of the lack of satisfaction with one's possessions, status, or situation. Sounds so familiar, doesn't it? Our circumstances just seem worse than others. Our possessions don't look as shiny or as plentiful. Our progress on the career ladder is going nothing like other people's is going. How can anybody be satisfied with this?

We can't, we say. And so the discontentment within our lives plays out in its many different ways. Jealousy, comparison, greed, feelings of insignificance, wishing for different skill sets or bodies or kids or husbands or jobs. We become people who can't see the value of what God is specifically doing in our lives, who can't see why we'd want to stay in the places where He's strategically positioned us. And the reason we can't see it is because of all the blurriness that gets in our eyes by looking around at what we *could* be, and *where* we could be, and why we'd be so much happier if we were.

None of us can skip through this chapter or this topic without being able to relate to it as a problem in our lives. Maybe you can't wait to get out of high school and truly start living. Or you can't wait till you get a better job than your current one. Or you can't wait till you have a ring on your finger or a baby in the extra bedroom. I've got my own areas of discontentment, and you've got yours.

But buckle up, baby, because I'm tired of it. And I'm taking it on.

———

As I've said before, I'm not naïve enough to think this problem of discontentment is a creation of the twenty-first century. Since the beginning of time, we humans have been dissatisfied with our circumstances. Open up God's Word and you'll see numerous examples of men and women struggling to be content with the lives they were living. Whether it included not enjoying their current status, their parenting journey, their spouse, or their ministry calling, we see it all, as far back as we can look.

In fact, why don't we just do that? Go back as far as we can look.

Let's start with Adam and Eve.

If you grew up in church, I think you'll recognize their story, but let me give you the CliffsNotes version. There was nothing in existence but God. Then God created the heavens, the earth, the stars, and everything we know to be in existence today. He also created humans. He made the man first, but He knew the man didn't need to be alone. So He

then created the woman to live with the man, to be his partner and complement him.[17]

Everything was perfect now. There was no sin, nowhere
in sight. The man and woman were in the garden with the
animals, enjoying their life and—who knows?!—maybe taking God at His word already and trying to procreate the earth.
But we do know Adam and Eve felt no shame, and they were
surrounded by everything they could possibly need. Life was
indeed *perfect* for them.

Let's pick up the story in Genesis 3 and see when things
took a turn for the worse for these two:

> Now the serpent was more crafty than any
> other beast of the field that the LORD God
> had made. He said to the woman, "Did God
> actually say, 'You shall not eat of any tree in
> the garden?'"

What we see here is Eve and a serpent having a conversation. I know it sounds a little weird, but the serpent was
actually Satan in disguise. He's a sneaky little guy, so when he
appeared in the garden, he was trying to convince Eve that
she misheard the commandment God had made to them,
where He'd said, "You may surely eat of every tree of the
garden, but of the tree of the knowledge of good and evil you
shall not eat, for in the day that you eat of it you shall surely

------

[17] Genesis 1 and 2 explain all this!

die." Those were God's exact words. But Satan tried twisting them around on Eve, implying that God said they couldn't eat from *any* tree in the garden.

Satan was planting a seed of doubt. He was trying to convince her that what God had given her wasn't enough, that His plan for her life wasn't the best it could be.

She knew in her heart the serpent was telling her a lie. That's why her first reaction was to defend God and the command He had given them. *No,* she said, *that's not right.* "We may eat of the fruit of the trees in the garden"—all except for one. "God said, 'You shall not eat of the fruit of the tree that is in the midst of the garden, neither shall you touch it, lest you die.'"

Right. She was mostly right. (Except that God didn't say they couldn't "touch" it, just that they couldn't eat of it. Not sure why she added that part.) This plan that God had set up for them gave them plenty of trees full of fruit they could eat from. It wasn't as if Eve was walking around the garden wondering what she was going to eat for the day. She wasn't wasting away from lack of nourishment. Her hunger couldn't possibly have gotten the best of her, not if she was choosing to live fully inside the generous provision God had made for her life.

The only thing that was able to get the best of her was this accusation coming straight from the lying mouth of Satan, the mistaken belief that God was holding out on her.

And the serpent knew it. And dug in.

> The serpent said to the woman, "You will not
> surely die. For God knows that when you eat
> of it your eyes will be opened, and you will be
> like God, knowing good and evil."

She could be like God? Could be her own God? Well,
okay, *that's* something Eve didn't have. God had given her
so much—more than enough to be able to live out her purpose, enjoy her life, flourish in community, and experience
the safety of His protection around her. And yet she wanted
more. The things she had, the things she'd been given, none
of them seemed like enough now.

> So when the woman saw that the tree was
> good for food, and that it was a delight to the
> eyes, and that the tree was to be desired to
> make one wise, she took of its fruit and ate,
> and she also gave some to her husband who
> was with her, and he ate.

Maybe that's why she added the thing about not touch-
ing it. Maybe the reason she went down so easily, with hardly
a fight, was because she'd already been up close to that tree.
She'd known she was drawn toward it, that she wanted it.
After all—this is the thing that gets me every time—it wasn't
a dead tree. It wasn't the ugliest tree in the garden. It wasn't
an outdated tree. It drew her eye because it seemed to hold
an enjoyment, an experience, that was better than what she'd

found in the life she'd been given, paradise though it was. She thought, *I could be wiser. I could be happier.* Because maybe God didn't really have her best interests at heart. Maybe Satan was right and God was wrong.

Maybe the something this tree offered was the something she was truly missing.

I suppose it's possible that Eve was just minding her own business that day when the devil came along. Maybe she was doing what she would have done on any other day (which I'm guessing was amazing because IT WAS THE GARDEN OF EDEN!!!) when Satan enticed her into believing something else must be better. Because, gosh, he is crafty and convincing.

But I think Eve perhaps was already becoming discontent with the fruit of all the trees she could eat from—just like how we grow discontent with the day-to-day normal of the trees we get to eat from. And she focused on the only one that didn't belong to her and wasn't best for her.

It's as if for a moment she forgot the fact that God had thoughtfully, intentionally put her and her man in a place where all their needs were met, that she was loved by God, that she'd been given anything good she might need. And yet Satan convinced her to focus on the one thing she couldn't have. Her desire for what wasn't hers cost her all the blessing of what she already had.

We know how this story continues. Once Eve and Adam had eaten the fruit, "the eyes of both were opened, and they knew that they were naked." Shame. Loss. Confusion. Disorientation. There was distance now in their relationship with God. Life wasn't the same anymore, now that a pure, perfect existence in Eden hadn't seemed like enough.

But I hope you don't shake your head and think Eve's blunder was one we wouldn't have made ourselves. Because we are the same. We'd have done the same thing. You and I are just like her, aren't we? We've all looked around at our circumstances and thought there must be something better than this. We've all thought there must be a better way to happiness. That's what Eve was doing.

> **Her desire for what wasn't hers cost her all the blessing of what she already had.**

It's what we do too.

God has put us in places and communities that matter. He has crafted our lives and our families with a purpose. He has given us talents, gifts, and passions. A voice. A calling. And yet we still find ourselves looking at it all and wishing it was different, wishing it was better.

Because if not even Eden was enough, surely these lives we live out here a long way from paradise can leave us feeling far less than satisfied.

It's a tale as old as time. But maybe it's time we changed the narrative.

———

Since discontentment is something we've seen in play since the very beginning, is there any hope for us today? Can we become content in who we are? In who God has made us to be? In the city He's placed us in? In the community where He's planted us? Can we be content using the gifts we've been given—*these* gifts, the ones that seem so small and insignificant by comparison—to serve those around us?

I've asked myself these questions before, and I have a suspicion you've had the same thoughts yourself. It's no surprise what discontentment does to our souls, our ministries, and our joy. So, of course we're on the lookout for the secret sauce to being content. But is becoming a person who is fully content even possible?

My answer is YES and NO.

You want the good news or the bad news first? I'll start with the bad news.

No, we will never be totally, 100 percent perfect in this life as far as contentment goes (or in anything, really). Sure, we'll be totally perfect at it *one* day, but not while we're still here on earth, am I right?

Sounds like such a bummer if you ask me, but it's true. We're all still human. We're all still broken people who will never completely outgrow our love for sinning. And though He can help us experience moments when we're truly walking in the freedom He's fought and won for us—even in the area of contentment—we won't be all the way there until the day He takes us home.

So, no, we don't ever get to fully escape the contentment struggle on this side of life. It will always be a struggle in certain seasons. Just will.

But the struggle itself is what leads to the good news. That's because, just a reminder here: struggling with something isn't necessarily a bad thing. It's always good to be in the fight. Struggling means you're not settling. Struggling means you're not giving up. You're striving. You're growing. And *growing* is what God has made possible for us, we who otherwise would possess no hope for achievement or advancement. To be steadily growing in contentment—struggling to be satisfied—is where I hope you find me every day, fighting for it and getting better at it in all of my circumstances.

But it's hard. I get it.

The reason why Paul is one of my favorite people in the Bible is because he was always so up front about his brokenness and his inability to follow Jesus on his own strength. That's what makes him feel so real to me, makes him feel normal. He sounds like he understood the struggle I face, trying to do what I know is right even if I sometimes mess up in doing it.

Paul said, for example, "I do not understand my own actions. For I do not do what I want, but I do the very thing I hate." I have so been there and done that, Paul. As in, *today* I have been there and done that.

You too? Ever been trying so hard to do the right thing but kept doing the wrong thing? You want to be content where God has placed you. You don't want to be jealous of others' positions. You don't want to compare your gifts or your ministry to everyone you see online. You want to believe that God is always doing what's best. You want to trust Him in all of your circumstances. You want to be happy with your own voice and calling. And yet you find yourself doing the very thing you hate. *Lacking contentment.* Constantly wishing your life could be different.

But Paul says you *can* grow consistently more contented. There *is* a way to make it happen. And here it is: The secret to being content is letting God be your strength for doing it.

> *"I can do all things through*
> *him who strengthens me."*

Now I'm sure you've never abused this Scripture, but I have. When I was in high school, I actually wore this verse on my letter jacket. Our school let us put our names on the back of our jackets along with a favorite phrase underneath, and I chose the "I can do all things through Christ" of Philippians 4:13 for mine. But the reason I can say I was abusing it is because I wasn't even following Jesus at the time, and yet I still wore that verse proud. Because, hey, I wanted to run faster in track, and make more baskets in basketball, and maybe even score a great boyfriend. That's what I wanted to do. And if Christ was offering me the strength to do those things—to do "all things"—count me in. "I can do all things through Christ who gives me strength," right? I can do it all!

But to understand what Paul meant here—about doing all things through Christ—we need to back up a bit and read the verses that come before. Understanding what the Bible is saying requires reading it in context, and honestly we need some context for Philippians 4:13. Because without it, Paul sounds like he's telling us we can count on Jesus always being on hand to help us do whatever we want in life, like Robin Williams as the genie in *Aladdin*. And yet the thing that Paul was giving God credit for doing in his life—the thing we can always be confident of doing "through him who strengthens me"—was what he'd discovered in Philippians 4:11.

> For I have learned in whatever situation I am
> to be content.

CONTENT. There it is—the word we're all desiring in our lives. Contentment. Paul said he had learned to be content in whatever circumstance he found himself. Which, side note here, Paul wrote this letter while he was IN PRISON! So not only was he letting them in on a secret he'd found, but he was telling them he'd found it while languishing in forced confinement.

I've never spent a night in prison, although I've spent time ministering to women who have. But I wouldn't need to be on speaking terms with a prisoner to know that the secret to finding contentment behind the bars of a jail cell should surely work everywhere else. So when Paul says, "I know how to be brought low, and I know how to abound. In any and every circumstance, I have learned the secret of facing plenty and hunger, abundance and need"—he's saying *that's* what we can do through Christ who gives us the strength.

There's our secret. And notice it doesn't depend on our circumstances.

Our world says contentment arrives in our lives when things finally start going well—when the job is secure, when the kids are behaving, when all your former problems become tied up in a nice, neat bow. Culture tells us that contentment is attainable by meeting our goals, realizing our dreams, basking in our success. We'd be content, we think, if we could ever find that peaceful place where everything settles down, where the pace is manageable, where people seem happy with us, and where we've got all the time we need for working our plan.

I'm thinking here of a review I read recently on a Taylor Swift album. I've never been a huge T-Swift fan—not because of anything I don't particularly like about her; I just haven't added her songs to my listening rotations. But the reviewer based his praise on her reaching "a point of contentment in artistic and personal self-perception—a confidence that comes with a steady near-decade-and-a-half ascension to the top." She'd worked hard. She'd made it. I mean, who wouldn't feel content with their life if they were succeeding at the level of a Taylor Swift?

But do you see anything wrong with this form of thinking after what we've just read in Philippians from Paul?

Most people equate contentment with success. They make contentment conditional on their circumstances. And yet as followers of Jesus, we see from God's Word that the secret to contentment is not success or power or happiness. It is only achieved through the strength God gives us for it, *regardless* of circumstances. Only through His promise of strength do we find contentment. And His strength is available at all times, under any conditions, no matter if those conditions are making you happy or if they're the most difficult ever.

When we get to a point in our lives that we TRUST GOD in such a way that we can look around at our lives, our mess, our pain, our joy, our good things—whatever!—and say, "I trust You, Lord, in all of this because I get my strength from You and You alone," that's when we'll finally start experiencing growth in our ability to be content.

We cannot drum up enough strength on our own for contentment in those seasons. We are simply not strong enough for it. But the strength of our Lord is.

In their book *God's Wisdom for Women*, authors Patricia Miller and Rachel Gorman describe contentment this way: "Contentment is not finally getting to a place of peace and rest when all is complete, accomplished, finalized, or safe. Contentment comes amid the mess and pressures of life— the quiet confidence and assurance that God is in control."

Sounds much easier said than done, am I right? It really is hard work. But it is *doable* work, we know, because we can "do all things" when we're pursuing contentment from a heart that's trusting in God alone.

———

All right, so maybe you're convinced now that your contentment can't be dependent on whether your life is smooth sailing or not (whatever "smooth sailing" means for you). And maybe you realize your ability to stay content is only possible because of the strength God provides you. *But how, Jamie? How do I do that?* You still want to know how.

Well, let's go back into the Word again, because God says that's where He's laid out for us "all things that pertain to life and godliness." And maybe we can find a little action verb in the Bible somewhere that'll help us make contentment a more permanent fixture in our hearts and in our daily thoughts.

Jesus said, "By this my Father is glorified, that you bear much fruit and so prove to be my disciples." I think we all as Christian women can say we'd be a lot more content if we knew we were producing the kind of fruit in our lives that our Father finds *glorifying*, wouldn't you agree? I mean, sign me up for that! Deep in my core I long to produce good fruit. I want it said of me that I'm a productive part of this kingdom that God is so focused on growing.

And by *fruit*, I'm thinking of the "fruit of the Spirit" that Paul talked about. In case you've forgotten what makes up that list or are just too dog-tired to go look it up right now, I'll spell it out for you from Galatians 5—"love, joy, peace, patience, kindness, goodness, faithfulness, gentleness, self-control."

We all want to produce these things, and we know we'd feel more content with our lives if we were producing them consistently. Here's the problem though. It's not enough just to *know* where our strength for bearing fruit and being content comes from. Because we forget. We grow tired. We get overwhelmed by our schedule, or a tragedy strikes, or someone else jumps ahead of us in line for something we really wanted, and all our trust in God's strength goes flying out the window. If we ever really expect to be content in Jesus, we need more than just our knowledge of His available strength. He said we need to "abide" in Him, in the source of all the good things in us.

Jesus spoke directly to this principle when He said to His disciples, "Abide in me, and I in you. As the branch cannot bear fruit by itself, unless it abides in the vine, neither can you, unless you abide in me."

So, there's your *how* word: ABIDE.

It's impossible for us to produce faithfulness, patience, peace, and all of the other fruits of the Spirit on our own. It's impossible for us to experience contentment with ourselves unless we're completely connected with Him. It's not just *kind of* hard. It's not only hard after we've done it for a while. Jesus says we cannot bear fruit AT ALL apart from abiding in Him. The Greek word for "abide" is *meno*, meaning "to stay (in a given place, state, relation or expectancy), to continue, dwell, endure, to be present, remain, stand." Jesus wants us dwelling in Him, continuing in Him, remaining in Him.

I know it sounds so elementary. *Of course* we want to dwell with Jesus. *Of course* we want to abide in Him. Yet so many times we don't do it. And the reason we don't—the reason you and I are maybe not abiding in Him right now—is because we're making our home in so many other places instead. In our fears. In our comforts. In our desires. And, yes, in our discontentment. Some of us have lived in discontentment for so long and have made ourselves so at home in it that we've hung pictures on the wall. We've got mail coming to that address. We've been living there with such regularity, *abiding* in it, that it'd take a crowbar to pry us out of there now.

We choose to dwell in our safety and comfort. We choose to dwell in our own power, in our futile belief that we can make ourselves better. We choose to dwell in our fears, in our worries, in the cocoon of our own plans and schemes. We choose to dwell in our own strength. And I'm sure you've noticed, as I have, that these things are no doubt failing you. They are unable to sustain you in this lifetime.

But Jesus said, "I am the vine; you are the branches. Whoever abides in me and I in him, he it is that bears much fruit, for apart from me you can do nothing." If we want to be women who produce something that matters, we need to be women who trust in what He says—that our only way to produce good fruit is to abide in Him.

I'm going to make a wild statement, and I could be wrong about it, but hear me out. I would guess that about 89 percent of the time[18] when we become discontent with the lives God has granted us, it's because we're not abiding in Him. We're abiding somewhere else. And it's just hard to trust God's best for your life when you're abiding in other things besides Him. You sure can't do it for long. Jesus is quite frank when He says that apart from Him you can do nothing—*nothing!*—just as a branch cannot bear fruit unless it's attached to the vine.

I'm the first to admit I don't have a green thumb. I've tried and failed at gardening many times. But there's one thing I do know. No branch or plant or twig on its own can ever produce fruit if it becomes severed from the main branch. It is physically impossible.

And we are the same as that branch. Apart from Jesus we cannot produce fruit. It's IMPOSSIBLE. We must abide, dwell, remain in Jesus in order to produce fruit.

One of the byproducts I've seen not only in my own life but also in the lives of other women is that in all our hustling

---

[18] I'm no statistician, and I have no idea where I came up with this number. I thought about saying 99 percent, but everybody says that.

to produce so many things, even good and godly things, we lack the strength that comes from abiding in the source of our strength. We're spinning our wheels trying to keep it all together, trying to make it all happen, convinced that all our work is surely leading us toward that elusive sense of satisfaction and contentment we crave. But we're striving to no avail. We're frustrated by how little fruit we produce that feels lasting and worthwhile. We see *others* producing fruit, which only makes us press into our work with more determination. But in essence we're trying to be like Jesus without *doing* it like Jesus, without doing it the way He's said is the only way to do it.

Interestingly, Jesus' command is not to bear fruit; His command is to "abide." You and I, we're often just striving for the fruit. We're chasing the good things we think we should be producing, the things we believe will make us more content as Christians, the things we see happening in others' lives and wish for ourselves.

But the command is simply to ABIDE. And when we abide, the fruit will follow.

Including the fruit of contentment.

You may be feeling crushed right now, full of anxiety, doubled over from the stress of not having what *she* has. But if you're more concerned with bearing fruit than with abiding in Jesus, you're missing out on how you produce true fruit in your life. And as a result, you're missing out on what it takes to be content.

Contentment comes from *God's strength* at work in your life, not from a certain set of circumstances or a certain color palette of experiences. And God's strength comes from *abiding in Jesus*, from going all-in on Jesus, which amazingly causes the fruit of contentment to grow like crazy in your heart, along with all the other things that make you most glorifying of the Father.

So, *abide*. Abide in Christ. And the fruit of contentment (along with a bunch of other things) will naturally grow. Take your eyes off contentment and put them on Jesus, and sooner or later you'll notice your heart is growing all sorts of good things you never saw there before!

Chapter 7

Unavoidable but Invaluable

The Opportunity in Adversity

I picked up my son from preschool early that day because our pediatrician had suggested I take him to see a specialist. The issue was with his voice, which—to be honest, was just the cutest little thing I'd ever heard. It had this delightfully raspy quality to it. And when he would be singing out loud and pretending to riff on the air drums, it was the absolute most darling thing a momma of a four-year-old could possibly imagine. It was so sweet listening to him.

But I couldn't help noticing, despite how adorable I found it to be, that his voice was growing more and more strained. Trying to hear him when he spoke was becoming harder for us. If he was seated behind me in our minivan, the only way I could comprehend what he was saying was by reading his lips in the rearview mirror.

So, realizing something else might be at play here, I mentioned it offhand to our pediatrician, who referred us to an ear, nose, and throat doctor.

That's where we were headed that day in the car, along with my two-year-old daughter, who I'd brought along with me. I had called the doctor's office the day before in hopes of getting an appointment after Christmas because, honestly, who has time between Thanksgiving and Christmas for doctor's appointments? But they said they had a cancellation and could work us in the next day. *Fine.* We'd go in, they'd check him out, we'd be on our way with a prescription or something, maybe a simple remedy involving stuff we already had in our pantry or the bathroom closet, and it'd be back to our expectant state of Christmas happiness.

There wasn't one sliver of fear in my mind about what I would hear from the doctor. I've been known to expect the worst from life, but everything seemed so normal that day. I hadn't even done a search of my son's symptoms online to scare myself to death with the worst-case possibilities. He had a little croak to his voice, that's all. Maybe they had a lollipop for it.

But had I known what the ENT was going to say to me, I wouldn't have gone there alone with my son. I'd have made sure my husband came along with us.

Had I known what I was about to hear, I would've left my two-year-old with a friend.

Had I known what was going to be said in that room, I would've asked someone to bring us dinner that night.

Had I known the words that were going to get thrown around that day, I would've canceled everything in my life for the next week to grieve.

But isn't that how tragedy and hard times enter into our world? They show up uninvited. You're rarely expecting them when they arrive. They're often the last things in the world you were ready for.

And I just wasn't ready for this.

Within minutes after the doctor had listened to my son speak and put a scope down his throat, he diagnosed him with RRP, which stands for Recurrent Respiratory Papillomatosis. RRP causes tumor-like lesions to grow on the vocal cords, and the only treatment is surgical removal. There's no cure. In fact without treatment it can become quite serious, to the point of being a potentially life-threatening disease.

There it was. That word. *Disease.* That word was now a part of our lives, and there was nothing I could do to put it back in the doctor's mouth. I now had a child with a "disease"—a named condition I could hardly pronounce, much less spell, that would send me scrambling to try and unearth all the research treatment options and success rates and everything else I could find on the subject of a medical condition I had no prior knowledge about.

I remember walking to the parking garage that day, looking at my unknowing four-year-old, and wishing I could walk back into that office and ask the doctor to switch the diagnosis to *me*. I wanted to be the one with RRP. I wanted the bumps on *my* throat. I wanted the surgery to be scheduled in two weeks for *me*. I didn't want my little four-year-old having to endure what the doctor said could potentially be ahead of us.

I called my husband and wept on the phone. Why was he not there with me? Why was I buckling my kids into their car seats without him, having to carry the weight of this diagnosis alone? Life was not feeling fair at all right then.

I imagine you know what that moment feels like, at least to some degree, perhaps to an even much, much larger extent. If you've lived any amount of life, you've most likely experienced a loss, sadness, or unexpected trauma of some kind. I'm guessing you've watched friends suffer or quite possibly have been the one enduring the suffering yourself. You've probably heard the word *disease* mentioned in reference to your loved ones throughout the years. You've probably had those moments of asking God why.

But this was a big one for me. It kicked off a series of surgical procedures: first every six weeks, then every eight weeks, then every twelve weeks. His last two surgeries were thankfully twelve months apart, nearly eight years ago now. Those were the last he's needed so far. But there's no guarantee he won't need another one. The disease is unpredictable.

And although we were told he was in "remission" after his last surgery, RRP continues to hang around my heart like an elephant in the room. I'm constantly wondering if God has healed him like we prayed, or whether we're just waiting until the papillomas strike again.

At some point during this long ordeal with our son, I read a book by author Michael Kelley where he recounts the journey their family undertook when his two-year-old son was diagnosed with cancer. He talks about how he reconciled what it means to believe in God despite a broken world where a little kid he loved so much had to endure chemotherapy. I devoured that book because I, too, was having some of the same fears, struggles, and thoughts about God myself.

I remember sitting in the waiting room during the seventh and final surgery, crying and asking God: *Why? Why us? Why him? Why now?* I was catapulting all these "whys" at God, who of course can take all our questions, and can take them all of the time. But Michael says, so wisely, "If we really want to start down the road of asking 'why,' let's not sell ourselves short of following it all the way to the end. At the end, there's God. He's the one in control. He's the only being in the universe that is sovereign. He's the beginning and the end of all things, including our laments."

The answer we don't want, and yet the only answer there can be, is that God has a why. He has not forgotten us or failed us, yet is with us and will use us to bring glory to

Himself somehow, whatever we must suffer in this life. Does it make sense all the time? Not to me.

But I believe this with all my heart. God is in control. I believe He has a plan. I believe He allows things to happen, even painful things, in order that they can become a cause for bringing deeper growth in us and more glory to Himself. In an interview with Beth Moore on my podcast, she said it so beautifully when talking about trials: "God made it matter." Some things in life are not worth it and we would never want to walk through them again, but we can say that God made them matter.

I write this all so easily, sitting here at a distance from it. But I also know what it's like to say it and believe it—to *want* to believe it—right there in the waiting room, where I was breathlessly anticipating results from another surgery. Yet in those times I wondered to myself if my heart would be able to follow what my head seemed to know—that when I am weak, He is strong; that when I am faltering, He is faithful to me.

Michael goes on to say:

> It's a journey of trying to embrace the fact that God is our refuge but not a comfortable one to hold on to. It's a journey of realizing that He is our safe place, and yet He is not safe at all. It's a journey of realizing more and more of what it means to walk deeply with

God and with all the doubt, fear, anxiety,
peace, and joy that come with it and how
those things can possibly coexist together.

Have you ever wondered how to walk out your calling in
the midst of all the doubt, fear, and anxiety that can come our
way? How can God use us for great, big, kingdom-changing
things in the midst of what seem like the worst moments of
our lives?

———

We carry around a false sense of security in our hearts
when everything is going right. We love that sense of control, as if we're holding all the pieces of our world together
through our own effort and can-do attitude. Then out of
nowhere a global pandemic enters our world and forces us to
face our lack of control over anything in our lives.

In fact I wonder if deep down we think suffering, trials,
and tragedy are things that only happen to the weak, that we
are stronger than others if we've managed to avoid it. I don't
think we'd admit to this idea as Jesus-loving ladies, though it
does cross our minds. I've interviewed hundreds of women
for my podcast, and many of them have endured suffering
beyond what I could ever imagine.

And let me tell you: they are not weaklings.

At first I was amazed by what I'd hear them say when discussing their trials—amazed at the strength they exude, at the passion of their love for Jesus, at the focus with which they follow Him. But now I've come to expect them to say these things. I'm almost surprised if they say anything different.

I hear Retha Nichole, for instance, tell how the circumstances that God allowed into her life, after finding out her husband had been having an affair—"this was all to save me," she says.

I hear Kate Merrick, who's joined me twice on *The Happy Hour*. Both times we've talked about the death of her daughter Daisy. It was quite possibly the hardest thing she'll ever walk through. It hasn't been easy. But the way she and her husband have journeyed through this tragedy has been nothing short of a picture of the gospel. As Kate said in her first book, *And Still She Laughs*, "I've learned not to fear suffering because it's not my enemy; it is my teacher."

I hear Rachel Henry, who's endured what many of us would consider one of our worst fears. Three men broke into her house one night while her husband was out of town, raping her as her children slept in their nearby bedrooms. When she shared her story with me, I was struck by her tenacity, her courage, her ability to talk about the worst night of her life. She talked about forgiveness and moving forward and still trusting God after this disaster struck her family.

I hear Lauren Scruggs Kennedy, who lived through a horrible accident where she somehow got too close to the spinning propeller of an airplane, severing her left hand and losing her left eye. She revealed to me how she doesn't view that moment as the worst thing that's ever happened to her or the worst thing in her life. *How?* I asked. "Well, it completely comes from the Lord," she said, "but there were certain nights when I would just wake up and be like, okay, I am so loved by the family around me. They're here for me in every moment. They're praying over me. They're pouring so much truth into me and Scripture and comfort." She's thankful for the nearness she's felt to God in the midst of her tragedy and how He's used the pain in her own life to help her minister to others.

I hear Amanda Brown, my friend who was given a dangerous heart diagnosis way before she'd even turned forty. Her future was in limbo. She wondered if she would live to see any of her boys graduate high school. Yet during those darkest days, during the heaviest conversations she had with her cardiologists, and all throughout the serious unknowns of that period, she says that's when she felt closer to God than ever before.

None of these ladies would ever wish for anyone else to endure what they've experienced. And I know they'd never want to walk through it again themselves. But what I do see in all of them is a realization that the things they've been through were not the result of anything they did or didn't do. It wasn't their fault. It's simply what God allowed into their lives, and He alone can make their suffering matter.

But they are different now because of their suffering. They love God more. They know Him in a deeper, more intimate way than they might ever have known Him if not for going through some of the worst days of their lives. Their seasons of suffering didn't destroy them. In fact, it might be how they truly became themselves. God walked them through difficulty and brought them out a different person—the person they were made to be.

These women have taught me what their suffering has taught *them*, that God is at work amid our pain. And in the weirdest way ever, I've learned that I can be thankful for the work He's doing in me, even when I'm hurting or upset.

Did these trials that entered their lives exempt them from usefulness? Did hard times have the power to put them out of commission? Did these women interpret their setbacks as signaling the end of their effectiveness in doing what God had called them to do? Whether from the guilt or pain or loss or disillusionment, did they conclude they had nothing more to offer?

No, when suffering became their teacher, God taught them who they were.

He showed them they were His.

I think this is one of the hardest parts of being a Christian. I mean, other things are hard too. There have been seasons of my life when abstaining from sexual immorality seemed like the hardest thing in the world to do. I think we can all admit to other times when trying to forgive someone who hurt us has proven enormously difficult. Jesus tells us we "cannot serve God and money" at the same time, that we must choose which one we desire the most, and we all know how difficult that choice can sometimes be.

But to look at our sufferings and think of them as producing something good in us is a difficult truth for me to wrap my brain around. To "rejoice" in my sufferings, like Paul says in Romans 5, seems counterintuitive to me. To see the "bad" things in my life and know they serve a purpose requires a level of maturity in my faith that I hope God is creating in me, even if I don't always feel like it.

But I guess I should just ask myself if I believe what the Bible says or not. Because James said, "Count it all joy, my brothers, when you meet trials of various kinds, for you know that the testing of your faith produces steadfastness. And let steadfastness have its full effect, that you may be perfect and complete, lacking in nothing."

Count it all joy? Yes, because God's Word is super clear that these "trials of various kinds" are producing something in us of enormous value. They grow our "steadfastness," a lifestyle of faithful endurance amid our troubles and afflictions. And steadfastness is what we want. We should crave being called steadfast. I know I do. I want to have an endurance faithful enough to get me through all my troubles and afflictions. I want to be faithful through whatever life throws my way.

And to hear the friends I've interviewed tell it, these "why God" moments have been where it finally happened for them. Their times of sorrow and tragedy proved this Scripture true. Their willingness to not give up, even when their right-there, right-then lives were so hard to deal with, has been the pathway God has used to produce something in them that they couldn't have gotten any other way. *Steadfastness.*

It's true. When I look back, for example, on that summer I told you about, when God called our family away from our happy, content, right-where-we-wanted-to-be life, He used those months of uncertainty and fear to grow something life-giving inside of me that wasn't there before, at least not to the extent or strength that I feel it now. I learned to trust Him more because of what we went through. I'm a different person today than before that summer started. I experienced His faithfulness in a fresh, new way—a hard, challenging way—and it galvanized me. It toughened me. It made me a little more *steadfast.*

And if that's what we truly want, we should start thinking of our trials differently. Rather than getting mad at how they've blown up our lives, at how they've gotten in the way of what we were doing—even when what we were doing, we thought we were doing for God—adversity is where He gives us a new opportunity to serve Him in another way. And to do it this time with more steadfastness.

My friend Katherine Wolf knows all too well what suffering feels like. She was a new mom, only twenty-six, living at the beach in California, when she suffered a massive stroke at her brain stem and woke up two months later to a severely disabled body and tremendous health problems. She spoke with me about her healing journey and the hope she's found in God throughout all of this.

It would be easy to look at Katherine's life today and wonder how she could continue serving God in her depleted physical condition. Think how many of the "big" things she'd planned for herself had surely all gone by the wayside now, impossible to contemplate anymore.

But that's not what you hear from her. She told me she *celebrates* where God has brought her. God has *called* her to this life, she says. God has redefined what happened to her that day and how she understands it, and she sees it altogether differently than how the world does. What we see as loss and restriction in her life, she now sees as God's special assignment for her. She has chosen not only to "live within the walls of suffering and survive there," she says, but to "celebrate and love my life from that place."

The world has taught us to run from suffering, to fiercely avoid it, to do whatever we can possibly do to prevent it from coming anywhere near us. And while I guess it would be a little unhealthy to *want* suffering or to go out looking for it somehow, there's still wisdom in expecting it. Even more, there's a deeper sense of purpose to be found in letting God take it and use it for whatever He wants to do with it.

Suffering may feel like weakness in our eyes, but in reality it is a highly useful tool in our spiritual growth.

What if we viewed suffering through the lens of the gospel? What if we didn't view it as a problem, as an anchor that dooms our success, as an indicator of how little we obviously matter to God? What if we viewed it instead as a direct companion to helping us get to the end of our days well?

My favorite verse in the whole Bible is, somewhat ironically, about suffering. (I've mentioned it briefly already.) I'm an enneagram 6, so I do tend to be on the lookout for the worst thing possible.[19] But the following set of verses are such a comfort to me in terms of what God can do in our lives through suffering. It's not that I'm asking for trouble, not at all. Nor do I feel like I'm a Debbie Downer, thinking I'm suffering all the time. It's just that I've lived a little more than four decades now, and I'm fully aware that nobody scoots through life without hitting some hard roadblocks along the way.

And so I join with Paul in saying to you, because of our trust in God's power, love, and grace, we can "rejoice in our sufferings, knowing that suffering produces endurance, and

---

[19] You know about the enneagram, right? Here's me: https://www. enneagraminstitute.com/type-6/.

endurance produces character, and character produces hope, and hope does not put us to shame, because God's love has been poured into our hearts through the Holy Spirit who has been given to us."

I want to stand up and start clapping every time I read these verses because I need this hope to hold on to. If my son's disease ever resurfaces, I need hope. If my marriage ever falls apart, I need hope. If one of my children passes away, I need hope. If I get breast cancer, I need hope. If my parents fall ill and move in with me, I need hope. Fill in the blank with your future suffering, and you too will need hope!

The reason we can rejoice in our sufferings is that the suffering is doing something in us. Suffering is creating endurance; endurance is growing our character; and the experience of seeing our character develop—the experience of seeing us truly become ourselves in God's hand—is a natural gateway to hope.

Trials and suffering are never pleasant, and I wish I could close my eyes, tap my feet together twice, and take away all of my suffering and yours. I can't. But I can lean in and trust God with the process, and I know I'll end up on the other side with hope—not just any hope, but a hope that cannot be put to shame!

And to think it all started with something I didn't want at all.

How's that for putting a positive spin on negative things? But really, that's not what I'm trying to do at all, just telling you to make the best of your bad situations. I'm not encouraging you to go back to the same life strategies you were employing before trouble came in and ran you off the road. As Courtney Reissig says:

> God is not in the business of "making the best of it" when things don't go our way. He doesn't just sweep in and pick up the pieces after our best-laid plans fall apart. He is always working, even in our disappointments, and using those trials for a greater purpose. So, we don't deal with disappointing circumstances by picking ourselves up by our bootstraps or turning our frown upside down. Rather, we trust in the God who is always working things out for our good.

The point is not to survive and advance, then to be more careful next time so that nothing like this ever happens to you again. The point is to accept trial and adversity as an irregular though inevitable pattern of life, and to choose to be faithful *through* it, not just around it.

What I've found in talking to other women and observing the trajectory of my own life is that we're either (1) soaking wet in the middle of a storm, (2) dripping wet on the other side of a storm, or (3) watching the next wave of storm clouds rolling in from out there on the horizon. I don't need to bring you any more stories to convince you that life will bring storms.

But I hope I've convinced you not to be scared of them. I hope I've convinced you not to work at building your life on a three-step strategy to outsmart the averages and prevent storms from ever showing up. There *are* no three-step strategies for staying dry through every rainy season.

God does, though, give us some advice in this regard. And, yes, it does require making some building plans.

Now we know that Jesus worked with his hands. Joseph, His earthly father, was a carpenter, so Jesus most likely learned some carpentry growing up. It's not unusual then, as He summed up His longest recorded sermon in the Bible (known as the Sermon on the Mount, found in Matthew 5–7), He used a house-building metaphor to represent our lives and to show us our need for a reliable spiritual foundation.

He used the example of two separate men who built their homes on two separate foundations. One of the men built poorly, on shaky ground.

> "Everyone who hears these words of mine and does not do them will be like a foolish man who built his house on the sand. And the rain fell, and the floods came, and the

winds blew and beat against that house, and it fell, and great was the fall of it."

The other man, however, built well.

"Everyone then who hears these words of mine and does them will be like a wise man who built his house on the rock. And the rain fell, and the floods came, and the winds blew and beat on that house, but it did not fall, because it had been founded on the rock."

Both men built a house.

Both men heard Jesus' words.

Both men endured rain, flood, and wind.

But that's where the similarities end. The chance of staying out of the storm was impossible. No one gets that option. But you and I do have a choice as to what kinds of foundations we'll choose to build—whether we'll *reject* the truth of God's Word and believe the world's definitions of success, or whether we'll *accept* God's Word as true and use what it teaches to face adversity well.

When we take our eyes off Jesus and start building our lives on our platforms, our audiences, our pride, our worth, our following, and our desires, we'll have nothing to keep us upright when trials hit. They'll shake us to our core because we've been working so hard to build our own foundation that we've hustled God right out of our lives. We've created something that can't ultimately support us. We'll end up thinking He's nowhere to be found and that our life has hit rock bottom.

But we have hope during the storm. Our hope is not built on the naïve notion that life will be easy and that we can muster up enough strength to overcome whatever comes our way. Our hope is not built on our own awesomeness, by thinking we can pull ourselves up by our bootstraps and create our own destiny. We'll only have hope in the storm when our lives are built on the right

> **We can work so hard to build our own foundation that we hustle God right out of our lives.**

foundation, when we don't see problems as dream killers but simply as God's next step in helping us become the strong, devoted, kingdom-focused people He's made us to be.

As Lore Ferguson Wilbert writes:

> In this life, we will have trouble. No bestseller from a cool Instagram mom or weekend conference with a man who says he's not your guru—but really, kinda, sorta is—will alleviate the trouble of living in a world groaning for full redemption. When we feel the pangs of the world we live in, instead of running to water that doesn't satisfy, empty wells, and

broken cisterns, drink deep from the Living
Water. Then go live in the body you have, with
the singleness you have, with the marriage you
have, with the kids you have, with the finances
you have—faithfully offering all of it back to
the one who awaits with perfection for you.

Or as pastor Tim Keller is known for saying, "If we knew
what God knows, we would ask exactly for what He gives."
I believe this to be true, and yet still I struggle with wanting
what God gives when it doesn't seem to be what I would
think is the best.

My son getting diagnosed with a disease
doesn't seem right.

Retha having to live through her husband's
betrayal doesn't seem right.

Kate losing her eight-year-old Daisy doesn't
seem right.

Rachel being tormented by strangers in her
own home doesn't seem right.

Lauren losing parts of her body in a terrible
accident doesn't seem right.

Amanda dealing with ventricular tachycar-
dia doesn't seem right.

Katherine having a stroke at twenty-six doesn't seem right.

Lots of things that you and I suffer don't seem right.

And yet God's Word promises us peace and hope when we trust in Him, even amid the unknowns and the worst days of our lives.

The writers of the Psalms knew what hard times felt like. It's what caused them to cry out so often, saying things like, "My God, my God, why have you forsaken me? Why are you so far from saving me, from the words of my groaning? O my God, I cry by day, but you do not answer, and by night but I find no rest." Their hearts, like ours, yearned to know if God was anywhere to be found during their most challenging times of struggle and hardship. And yet they could bravely say in the next breath, "You are holy, enthroned on the praises of Israel. In you our fathers trusted; they trusted you, and you delivered them. To you they cried and were rescued; in you they trusted and were not put to shame."

Even in their despair, they remembered that He is a God who has proven Himself trustworthy, and so they could trust Him amid their uncertainty. One minute they'd be wondering how something so terrible as this could happen, but then the next minute they'd be singing, "Your way, O God, is holy. What god is great like our God? You are the God who works wonders."

I have discovered in life that fear and peace *can* coexist. Sadness and hope *can* live together. How? Because God, who can do anything—God, who knows what we feel and think and can possibly endure—proves Himself faithful in the midst of our scary seasons.

I'm not one to pray asking God to send tribulations and sorrow into my life, but I am one to tell Him that I want whatever it takes to make me love Him and trust Him more. I want my life to matter—the easy parts as well as the other parts, the ones that cause me to curl up in a ball and scream my eyes out in frustration. I want this life of mine to be set apart and point a world in desperate need of a Savior to the One who can save them. I want God to use all of my life to bring Him glory.

And I want you and I to be a generation of women content in our trials, knowing that He is working all things in our life for His glory and our good.

Part III

Becoming
Yourself

Chapter 8

Bloom Where You're Planted

A few years ago my boys were trying out for football at their school. And depending on how well they performed in practice, they would each be selected to play on either the A-team (the best team) or the B-team (the second-best team). Some schools are so big that they even have a C-team. Know how I know? Because one of my boys spent his seventh-grade season playing on the C-team.

Now I can say as their momma, I could not have cared less about which team my kids were selected to play for. I spent all my middle-school years on the B-team in basketball, and I turned out just fine. Not once in adulthood have I ever grieved my fate as a B-team basketball player.

So while my boys certainly felt differently about it than I did—they obviously wanted to make the A-team, and I wanted it for them as well (because *they* wanted it)—all I really cared about was that they ended up on the *same* team. Because while I know there are worse things to endure in life than what I'm about to say, and while I like to watch football as much or more than anybody I know, I would much rather spend only *two* hours at the ball field than *four*.

But enough about me. Let's keep the focus on the kids, shall we?

That's why I was so glad, during the parents meeting, when the coach told us something he'd been telling the boys who were trying out, and I haven't stopped thinking about it since that day. No matter what team they ended up being placed on, he said, he expected them to do their best, to (in his words) *bloom where they were planted*.

"Bloom where you are planted," he'd been telling my sons. I even pulled out a piece of paper and scribbled those words down so I'd remember them.[20]

That's because sometimes you can't control where you land, just like my boys couldn't control which team the coaches chose for them, any more than I could control

---

[20] If you knew the number of papers I have in pockets, purses, books, etc., where I've scribbled things down, you would politely introduce me to the Notes app on my phone. I know it's there. I just really like a pencil and paper. (And sometimes I even remember where I put them.)

whether my weekly schedule would need to accommodate one game or two. But they could *bloom where they were planted*. They could play their hearts out on whatever team they were part of, whether it was the A-team or the B-team.

We can always choose to bloom, right where we're planted.

———

There's a lot of talk in our world today about choosing your destiny, about making yourself great, how if you don't like your circumstances, you have the power to change them. And while I'm all about hard work and striving, I do want to scream when I hear such statements as these.

I recently came across a video of a woman giving a pep talk to her followers, and I found myself sucked in by it and hanging on every word she said. For two and a half minutes or more, before I snapped myself out of it, all I could seem to think about was how if I started doing the steps she was laying out, my life would maybe start to look a whole lot more like hers. She made me feel as though I could do really big things for the world, for my career, if I would just work harder, if I would do the things she was telling me to do.

The only problem with this pep talk is that my life looks *nothing* like hers. I have four kids, for one thing. And each one of them has his or her activities outside of school. I have a career that includes travel, and I work from a tiny house on my property with no office manager. My husband is a pastor and songwriter who happens to travel a good bit as well. We do our own laundry, get our own oil changes, and even cook our own food—probably unlike the lady in that video.

I truly do want to be successful like her. And I don't think there's anything wrong with that. But can I be honest with you for a second? I think our culture has confused success with money. I think we've confused success with status. I think we've confused success with followers.

Can I be a bit *more* honest with you? I think I've confused success with some of those things myself, at certain times in my life.

I absolutely want to be successful at everything I do, whether in my parenting, my marriage, my career, or whatever else. I have a feeling you do as well. I don't want to fail at anything. I like putting my best foot forward in everything I do. But really, if I'm thinking more clearly and with less selfish ambition, all I actually want to do is "bloom where I am planted." Or, to borrow a word I've used throughout this book, I want to be *faithful.* Faithful with what God has given me. Faithful where God has placed me. Faithful to the people that God has put in my life.

Can I tell you a few ways where I think we're prone to confuse success and faithfulness?

Success = all your kids loving Jesus their whole lives because you raised them right

Faithfulness = pouring into your kids and understanding the result is not up to you

Success = creating a product that sells a lot and causes you to become "known"

Faithfulness = creating a product you're proud of supporting and standing behind

Success = winning "Woman of the Year" in your industry or community

Faithfulness = showing up for your community in the ways God has gifted you

Success = marriage plus children before you turn forty

Faithfulness = serving God whether alone or with a family

Success = building a platform that gives you access to a wide audience

Faithfulness = serving the ones that God has already given you influence over

When we idolize another person and what their version of success looks like, we create a standard that is not only unreachable but, honestly, just doesn't apply to us.

I'll give you an example. Imagine a woman who, for whatever reason, works outside of the home. Maybe she loves her job and feels a great purpose in what she gets to do. Or maybe her family couldn't survive without her income. Or maybe she's the one who brings in the most money while her husband is the one who stays home with their children. The reason doesn't really matter for my little illustration here. But if I've determined in my mind that a successful mother is defined as a woman who stays home with her children, I've not only created a standard that isn't reachable for many women in our world, but I'm proposing that *my* idea of success is the only *correct* view of success.

I've defined success by something other than faithfulness.

And I'm through doing that. A woman who is faithful to what God has pressed on her heart is a successful one. The woman who listens to what God asks her to do for her career and her family and obeys Him is the successful one.

I immediately think of my friend Jenn as a faithful woman. She designed the logo for my podcast and has helped me think through many dreams of mine—not just mine but a whole lot of others. She aptly calls herself a "dream defender" for the women she works with through a ministry she runs called Camp Well,[21] which helps women recognize their dreams and make them a reality.

I remember the first time I met her. We enjoyed bowls and bowls of chips and salsa and talked as if we'd known each other forever. We dreamed up a project over lunch that day which, even though we still haven't accomplished it, I think it's a great one, and I hope someday it jumps off our pile of ideas and becomes a living, breathing reality.

One thing that sets Jenn apart from many other women today is that she's made a conscious decision not to have children, to not become a mom. And I'll be honest with you: when I first met Jenn, I didn't fully understand this decision. I've dreamed of being a mom since I was a little bitty girl, and I assumed without thinking that every other little girl had this same dream as well. But I've learned from Jenn and a few others of my friends that it's a naïve statement to make, painting success for a young wife with only one color of brush.

Hearing her talk about it recently on Annie Downs's *That Sounds Fun* podcast reminded me of things Jenn had told me before. God had shown her years earlier that His plan for her life didn't include children, even before she was married for fifteen years in a destructive relationship that, despite all her fighting for it, eventually ended in divorce. Looking back, she said she's wondered if God was sparing her "children"

---

[21] Check it out at https://thewellsummit.com.

from the pain of going through their parents' divorce. Maybe so. But she was always 100 percent clear that children would not, indeed *could* not save her marriage.

Fast-forward a number of years, where Jenn found herself in love again, this time with her now-husband Rhett. She wasn't sure how he would feel about a forty-one-year-old divorced woman who never wanted children, but I'm happy to announce that they are happily married, and God hasn't changed her mind or feelings in regard to having kids.

Yet if you've been reading along and still feeling a little judgmental toward Jenn and her position on not having a family, see if this changes your mind.

A few years after moving to northwest Arkansas to start her new life with Rhett, tragedy struck a member of her newfound community. One of their dear friends, Zac, was killed in a motorcycle accident. And in one of the most selfless examples of friendship and love I have ever seen, Jenn has completely given herself to Zac's wife, Kelly, to help meet her needs during this horrific season of suffering. Jenn has become like family to Kelly, spending hours and hours just being with her, whether it's been playing with Kelly and Zac's son or helping out with everything and anything at a moment's notice, even including them in her family vacations.

In the podcast with Annie, she shared that God had given her, though many years ago, a single word to claim when He'd impressed on her heart that she shouldn't have kids. His word for her was "available." And though she couldn't possibly have known in those early days of womanhood how this word would play out in her life, God's plan has become abundantly clear for Jenn. She has been completely *available* to her friend throughout Kelly's entire grieving process, more available than she could possibly have been if she were caring for her own kids at home.

And so this opportunity has helped her see that God's plan for her—for *her*—was the best one. And I can't help but smile when I think about it. Her life has been purposeful and meaningful. *Successful,* I'd say—in ways that some people would tell you she couldn't or shouldn't be. But she has taken her circumstances and leaned into what God has shown to be her calling. And she has been faithful to that.

I look at Jenn's life today, and I see her redefining what success looks like in so many ways. She's not concerned about followers, or building a brand, or selling more of her books, or improving her destiny. She's simply concerned with being available to her friends, blooming where she's been planted.

And I call that success.

I hear a common sentiment from women today. They want bigger and better. Again, hear my heart here. I want to do better too. I want to reach more women. I want to grow my opportunities. The problem arises, however, when we yearn for a different bigger and better *right now* than the people that God has put right here in front of us, right this moment, to serve and love. When that yearning for a bigger and better influence discounts what God has given us today, or when bigger and better is defined by an unattainable standard, that's when we start veering off track.

Let me put it to you this way. When you're looking at the influence that God has given you—whether it be the three people who live in your home, or the eight thousand people who follow you on Instagram, or the twelve ladies in your office, or the eighty-three students you teach, or any other person who's right there in front of you—and you despise them because you want bigger and better than that, your heart may have a problem.

Perhaps you cringed at that word *despise*, but I used it on purpose. I think that's what we do whether we know it or not. We look down on and devalue the people who are already in reach of our voice, placing greater value on those phantom, unknown people who don't even exist. We begin to think that we're not making an impact because the number of people we have influence over is rather low in our opinion. Anytime we put hard figures on our actions, we develop an altered view of

> **The quality of your influence matters more—*much* more—than the quantity of your influence.**

what success and calling look like, because the quality of your influence matters more—*much* more—than the quantity of your influence.

My friend Jenn is not yet writing books on how to walk with people through grief, although she may write that book someday. But she is faithfully walking with her one friend, and she's making a difference right where she lives.

Another friend, Andrea, influences college students every semester. It might look like just a job to some, but to her it's an influence over those few young women that God has placed in her path.

My friend Amy never would have imagined herself running a therapeutic horse-riding and respite organization.[22] But sixteen years ago, God blessed her with Mabry, a daughter who has special needs. Amy's influence is not worldwide, but she is definitely changing the lives of forty-five adults each week who struggle in mind and body and find healing comfort through active engagement with animals. The quality of Amy's influence reaches a magnitude that some of us could only dream of.

Blooming where we're planted isn't just for seventh-grade boys wanting to play football in the fall. It's something for all of us to remember in our lives.

------

[22] I think you'd love finding out more about it at https://blueskytexas.org.

When we get down to the nitty-gritty of blooming where we're planted, I think some of us are confused about why we're planted in this particular spot. We might think we have a better idea of where we could be used.

When I was in my late twenties, we lived in a suburb outside of Nashville, and my husband traveled all the time, as I've said. When I say *all the time*, I mean all the time! It meant Momma was solo parenting a lot of days in a year.

I remember one particular weekend when I became thoroughly convinced my life was just not what I had planned it to be. I'd started to compare my life to Aaron's, and I wasn't happy with the part I'd been left to play, being alone with my kids while my husband was out having the most fun of his entire life. Without me. (Again, I lean toward dramatic when describing my feelings!)

He was staying in hotel rooms, while I was lying in our bed under sheets that hadn't been washed in who knows how many weeks. He was eating out in restaurants while I was eating chicken nuggets, peas, and peaches for dinner most nights. He was needing to buckle only his individual seatbelt every time he went out to drive, while I was wrangling two toddlers into car seats every time I had to go somewhere. He was sleeping entire nights without anyone waking him up, whereas I was interrupted from my slumber many nights for water or because of a scary dream or a "monster" under the bed.

Now let's be fair, which I tried to be. Yes, my husband was in a band traveling all those days, which is true. But I can guarantee you he would've chosen being home with me rather than sleeping on clean sheets in a new hotel room every weekend. I can guarantee he would've chosen chicken nuggets, peas, and peaches with his family instead of eating at a table full of dudes. He would have always chosen to be with us if he had the choice.

But he was living exactly where God had planted him, just as I was living where God had planted me, even when all I could see was hard and difficult and different from what Aaron had. I would daydream about putting on a power suit and walking into an office full of windows on the twelfth floor of a building and GETTING STUFF DONE. But in reality, I was walking to the kitchen in my pajamas at 2:00 p.m. to heat up my coffee for the fourth time that day and probably getting nothing done!

One Sunday when I'd taken my boys to church alone (again) because Aaron was out of town, I came home having one of *those* days. I was grouchy. I was certain God had forgotten me. I was tired. I was lonely. I was looking all around instead of right in front of me.

I was sitting on the porch of the first house we ever owned, watching my boys play together on the swing set in the backyard. They were having so much fun because that's what kids do even when their parent is stuck in her own pity party. But Aaron was on the road and my attitude was less than par. I was jealous of his hotel room, jealous of his meal at a restaurant, jealous of his quiet. Jealous of everything that I thought was better than my current reality.

But right there in the middle of my pity party for one, it was as if my eyes were instantly awakened and I realized what was right in front of me. My boys. My babies. My people. I stared at them through eyes that only a moment before had been seeing only duty and diapers and dishes to clean up. And as tears trickled down my cheeks, God adjusted something within me. For a sweet moment I looked at my situation through a new lens.

I began to think this way: I GET to see them every day. I GET to pour into them every day. I GET to read them stories every evening at bedtime. I GET to comfort them in the middle of the night. I GET to hold them when they're tired. I GET to nourish their bodies with meals three times a day and snacks five hundred and thirty-nine times a day!

I have never forgotten that moment.

It was so vivid, so redefining.

It may not sound like much as you read about it, but I cried that afternoon like I hadn't cried in a long time. I repented of my ugly thoughts and heart, and I begged God to remind me that my influence was huge and substantial right where He had me. Yes, the thought of being out of town and using my influence the way my husband was doing it looked mighty appealing at times. But it wasn't where God wanted me, and that meant it wasn't where I should've wanted to be at that moment either.

And I think we can all stand that kind of course correction every now and then.

At that time in my life, God had planted me alongside two little boys that I got to be home with and influence every single day. At other times in my life, it's been all four of my kids at home with me. At other times it's been a classroom full of eighth-grade students in a yearbook class.[23] At other times it's been a room full of fifth-grade girls in a Sunday school room. Today it's being a mom to my four kids in a way that looks different than it's ever looked before. And I expect it'll be different year to year, decade to decade, just as sometimes it's different day to day.

> **My ability to succeed in life is not determined by the number of people I influence; it's only determined by how well I steward the influence I've been given.**

---

[23] Yes, I was once responsible for the eight-grade yearbook in my first teaching job out of college. I also coached the middle school volleyball teams, even though I'd never played a day of volleyball in my life!

But my ability to succeed in life is not determined by the number of people I influence; it's only determined by how well I steward the influence I've been given.

Serve where you are.

Because those people matter.

And God has a purpose in putting you there.

Charles Spurgeon said it this way:

> God has made you what you are, a mother, or a daughter . . . serve God as such. There is something for you to do in your position. Extraordinary calls may come and I pray they may come to some here present, but they are not likely to be given to those who cannot use their present everyday opportunities. We may be called to very special service and have special Grace given, but it is best for us, till such calls are felt, to mind our business in the station of life in which God has placed us. Moses kept sheep until he was bid to deliver Israel. Gideon was threshing when the angel appeared to him. And the disciples were fishing when Jesus called them. They used diligence in their callings and then threw their hearts into their higher calling.

Let me repeat that last line in case you missed it.

*"They used diligence in their callings and then
threw their hearts into their higher calling."*

I can't help but think how many times we focus our eyes
on everything around us except for what's right in front of
us, right where God has put us. We want bigger and better,
but we aren't diligent with what's been given to us. We want
more followers, and yet we don't see the blessing in the ones
we currently have. We want a new life, and yet we aren't willing to diligently serve the people in the life we have today.

That's no way to be successful.

It's surely no way to be your best self.

—————

I surprised Aaron with a getaway for his fortieth birthday.
I had every intention to pack his bags and take him to the
airport without his even knowing about the trip, but I also
knew this was a sure way to evoke unnecessary anxiety on
a person. I presented Aaron with a card on a Friday night
telling him we were leaving on Sunday after church for a
birthday celebration. I told him what kind of clothes to pack
and that we were getting on an airplane and then renting a
car. That's all he knew.

We arrived in Phoenix and began a few hours' drive
toward our final destination of Sedona. Along the way, we
talked, listened to music, and admired the scenery that

looked so different to what we were accustomed to seeing in central Texas.

One thing I noticed were the ginormous cacti along the road, the kind with the big arms, the ones you want to stop and take your picture in front of. They're called *saguaro* cactus, and they can grow to more than forty feet tall. They are HUGE. And, oh, so strikingly beautiful. I'm now wishing I would've gotten out and made Aaron take my picture in front of one!

But the closer we got to Sedona, I started to notice we were seeing fewer and fewer of them. Whereas they'd once been almost everywhere we looked, now I saw mostly the smaller kinds of cactus that grow closer to the ground. The desert prickly pear, for instance, is beautiful in its own way, but they are for sure a lot different than those enormous cactus plants I'd been admiring along our drive.

A few days later we took a pink Jeep tour through the mountains, where our guide brought up the difference in cactus he said we'd probably seen as we drove up to Sedona. I immediately felt like Student of the Year for picking up on this fact earlier. He said the reason we hadn't seen any of the big, tall saguaro cacti up here in northern Arizona is because they can't survive there. Temperatures occasionally drop below freezing in that region, and the saguaro is so tall and full of so much water that it would freeze and topple over from its own weight. They were never meant to thrive in another type of climate than the one they thrived so amazingly in.

A light bulb went off in my head at that moment. Because isn't that descriptive of what we do? We go around wanting to be the big saguaro cactus, the one that looks so much better and shows off so much cooler in the pictures. We look around at other jobs, other women, other families, other careers, other gifts, other talents, and wish they were the ones *we* had or were more like. We think we'd be better off if we changed jobs, got married, married someone else, stayed home, worked outside the home, or moved to a new town. And yet sometimes we need to realize we weren't ever meant to thrive in those places or with those people.

God was so smart when He placed the saguaro cactus in southern Arizona where it can stand tall in its environment all year long. And He is so smart to place you and me in the places that are ideal for us as well, ideal for what we need and are able to offer.

I'm convinced we often miss the blessings that God has placed right in front of us because we think something better is out there for us. We've become so self-focused about our lives that we are no longer serving but are constantly trying to figure out how we can be served. We're comparing everything we have to everyone around us. We grow discontented with the gifts that God has poured out to us. We question our seat at the table. We wish we were invited to other tables rather than the one where we're seated. We look around and wonder why she has the life she lives and why we're stuck here with this one.

It's time we learned to bloom where we're planted. It's time we showed up where we've been assigned. This doesn't negate any amount of hard work and striving to do our best. But it completely negates hard work and striving for something that God never intended us to have. It means we trust in our seasons. We find peace with wherever God is using us. We quit wishing for someone else's life and begin living the one we've been given.

Paul said it this way:

> For we are his workmanship, created in Christ Jesus for good works, which God prepared beforehand, that we should walk in them.

Trust the God of the universe in what he has prepared for you. Walk in step with Him, trust in Him, serve Him, give your life away for Him, and watch your life bloom where He has planted you.

Chapter 9

Between Doing
and Being

I looked in the mirror and didn't like who I was becoming." My friend said these words to me through tears in her eyes. She had worked at a church for years, writing incredible Bible study curriculum. She'd encouraged me in my own writing as well. I saw Jesus all over the work she did—not just the quality of what she accomplished, but the heart with which she did it. Just an amazing person.

And here she was, telling me she was quitting her job, not because she hated her boss, not because she wasn't qualified to perform it, but simply because she'd seen something in herself that she wasn't happy about, something that had been disturbing her.

She didn't like who she was "becoming."

I was stunned at that statement. Because to me, simply looking in from the outside, I would've said she was doing exactly what God had asked her to do, being exactly who He had called her to be. And yet she somehow knew differently. She was so self-aware that even though she was working really hard on valuable things, she knew she was losing something valuable on the inside. She was losing her love for God. And she wanted to get it back, even if it meant stepping away from a job in Christian ministry that she was doing so well.

As one beloved Puritan prayer puts it, "I wish not so much to do as to be, and I long to be like Jesus." Our world puts a lot of focus and emphasis on what we *do*. But I wonder if in being so consumed by what we're doing, we're failing to ask ourselves the question that would help us gauge whether we're truly succeeding in life or not.

In spite of what you're doing, who are you *becoming*?

We've spent a lot of time together over these pages talking about our calling, our seats at the table, about our voices being used for His glory. We've talked about battling comparison and discontentment, trusting God through our trials, serving Him where He's planted us. A lot of good things to think about and deal with.

But I believe asking ourselves this one particular question—"Who am I becoming?"—could really guide us in our journey toward a more resolute faithfulness. I think we could save ourselves years of regret if we were to focus more on who we're becoming instead of being so inordinately consumed with what we're doing.

Who, I ask, would you say you're becoming?

———

I was talking with a friend recently about this exact topic. I often wrestle with how much is enough. When does the hustle just get to be too much? When am I hustling so much that I've ended up hustling God right out of my life, right out of my day today? She and I were trying to think of ways we could take inventory of our lives at those times when we can sense ourselves tottering off balance so that we could see what's likely causing it, could see what's really the matter, and could then see how to prevent it. More importantly, see how we could get ourselves back in our sweet spot of serving Him again, doing work that overflows from a heart growing every day more in love with Him.

I need to tell you ahead of time: this is a vulnerable conversation. If you dare to enter it and invite someone else into it with you, know that you will get your toes stepped on. You will feel defensive when things are brought to the light. You'll want to push back and make excuses. But I believe if we're open to allowing these friends of ours, people we trust with our hearts, to speak into our hustle, we'll all be better women for it. Our lives will begin to align more squarely with what we truly want ourselves to be.

And I think that's what you and I both desire. You want your life to matter for more than just *you*. You want to show off Jesus more than yourself. You realize from experience that if you're not careful with who you're becoming, you're liable to just hustle on ahead without Him. And the chances of that approach to life ending well . . . it's not just slim. It's none.

As my friend and I talked, we came up with a few litmus tests that we think indicate whether our hustle is focused on God instead of ourselves, allowing Him to stay in charge of who we're becoming, or whether we've set Him off to the sideline, making Him a casualty of our headstrong attempts to accomplish what we must think is more important than following Him.

Our discoveries seemed to gravitate into two categories: *Soul Care* and *Community Care*.

Soul Care: How's Your Time with God?

In order to become who we want to become, the Bible says we need to be "increasing in the knowledge of God." And in order to know God, we must spend time with God. There's simply no way around it. And no one else will do it for us.

I'm not talking about becoming a theological genius; I'm talking about becoming a woman who is persistently growing "in all spiritual wisdom and understanding," whose mind is being increasingly shaped more by the eternal realities of heaven than by the flimsy, flighty priority systems of this world.

You've heard the example a million times, but I think it's worth repeating. I can know just about every single thing about my husband—the details of who he is, the various lines that fill out his bio sketch. But unless I spend *time* with him, I won't ever truly know him. I'll never get any deeper than a factual basis. I'll keep my perceptions of him stuck in the past and not actively developing. If I truly want to know who Aaron Ivey is, I need to talk to him, be with him, listen to him, seek to understand him.

Why should it be any different with God? If I want to know how He thinks, if I want to know what His character is like, and if I want to know how His plans and purposes influence the way I follow Him—how they change the person I'm actually becoming—I need to make sure I'm spending a lot of time in His Word, a lot of time with Jesus on my mind.

Now if you grew up around church, I bet your thoughts are already turning to what Christians have long called their "quiet time"—a set-aside portion of the day when we get out our Bible and our prayer list or a devotional book or something, and we turn our attention to private worship and reflection. And, hey, I'm all for quiet time. We each have a tendency to fill up our lives with whatever's most pressing or most exciting at the moment. So we definitely stand to benefit from building planned appointments with God into our schedule, times where we force ourselves to stop, slow down, and be still before the Lord.

This is actually just common sense. We all recognize the value of creating structure in our day, of building frameworks around which all our other stuff (the less important stuff) needs to either find its place or wait till later. Like, if we didn't have a plan for things like doing our regular chores or scheduling a dental appointment or cleaning the bathroom or whatever, we would constantly put them off in favor of doing other things, more impulsive things, the kinds of things we find more fun and entertaining.

Let's just say I know this to be true.

Jesus did this kind of prioritizing. He valued getting alone with His Father. It wasn't because He was a weird hermit who avoided society at all costs; He simply knew He needed rest and peace if He was to accomplish what God had planned for Him. He knew He needed communion with His Father if He expected to be strong against temptation or remain sensitive to the heart's cry of others.

Because, look, He had the same tugs on His gut that we experience today. He got tired and wanted to sleep. He got hungry and wanted to eat. He saw opportunities for ministry happening around Him and felt the pressure to keep going and giving, way past the point where His human capacities could go and remain healthy. But He was keenly aware that *doing* and *being* were not synonymous terms. In order to keep serving, He knew He needed the anchor of letting His Father tend deeply to His soul.

So, quiet time? That's a good thing. A good thing to *do* that impacts who you *become.*

Now it'll obviously look different at different stages of life, but it still needs to be part of *every* stage of life. Otherwise, the repeated absence of it from your usual habit is telling you something. It's telling you that busyness and activity are more central to your heart than discovering God's real plan for all this activity in the first place. Your faithfulness in spending regular intervals with God—in letting Him take care of your soul—can be a major indicator that you're becoming more like Him.

But with that said, I think it's fair to say this too: Don't get so obsessive about having your quiet time that it becomes little more than a source of guilt and rigid checkmarks. The whole point of what I'm talking about—the whole point of seeing our need for time with God—is to view not just a daily devotional minute but the *entirety of our lives* as an ongoing opportunity to become more like Him in thought, word, and action.

Where, then, are you spending your time—all of it— all 168 hours of it each week? And how much of it are you spending on things that tend to the health of your soul?

I realize even these 168 hours per week can feel fleeting and limiting. I know how few of them can end up being left over to put toward your passions. I know you want to maximize every moment. And you should! I know you want to work hard, and you should. I know you may want to fill each crevice with activity and investment: another podcast to learn from, another online search for information, another article on someone else's methods and routines and their motivating steps to success. That's often fine too.

But ask yourself: Who are you really becoming when God gets so little of your time? Who are you becoming when it's been ages since you took a quiet walk without your earbuds? Who are you becoming when you spend more hours on Instagram and YouTube than in Ephesians and 1 John? Who are you becoming when you seem to have time for everything and everyone else but rarely if ever any time for the Maker of your soul?

Soul care may be a catchy term. But you and I will not become who we want to become in life if we're not letting God minister to our souls. It's often the first thing we let go when we're dreaming big dreams and hustling to make them all happen. But we won't be happy with the woman we're turning into if we're consistently failing to cultivate what's going on inside us.

Community Care: What Are You Experiencing with Your Friends?

Community can be as much of a buzzword as soul care, where we overuse it or discount it, diluting most of its meaning away. We hear it mentioned and talked about so often that we can start to lose an appreciation for its real value. But I'm here to suggest that *community* is one of the greatest assets the Lord has given us in helping us walk out this life.

The importance we place on community will tell us whether we're becoming our best self or not.

Often when we're striving to do more, we start pulling away from other people, not letting them truly engage with us, not spending as much time with them, not keeping ourselves in those places where we can learn from what they're saying. Have you noticed this happening in your own life? Are you becoming more isolated than before? Are you lacking in caring for others and being cared for by them? Do you have any space in your life anymore for feedback and constructive criticism? Have you invited trusted people into your inner circle and permitted them to call you out when your eyes have grown more fixed on success than on faithfulness?

God has put people in our path to bless us, to encourage us, to hold up a mirror to us, and just to plain link arms with us and go through life together. People matter. But we have a tendency to forget this. We easily bury ourselves in more measurable tasks, in our daily bullet points, in the lines of connected dots that take us from Point A to Point B. Again, I realize we can't carry out our callings faithfully without putting some real work behind it. But all these checklists of ours that help take us forward can also conspire against us to cancel real relationships right out of our lives.

And that's a problem—a bigger problem than it may seem. We are not our best on our own. We are not the most accurate evaluator of who we're actually becoming. We hide too easily in our own blind spots.

But not when we're living in ongoing community. In authentic community, others see through our blind spots.

Think back with me to the three types of people I mentioned in my earlier chapter on the parable of the talents: (1) the person who's faithfully utilizing their talents in serving people; (2) the person who's often dissatisfied with themselves because of comparing their abilities and opportunities with others; and (3) the person who's scared to step out and put their gifts to work outside their comfort zone.

The biblical mandate, of course—regardless of which of these descriptors more closely applies to you—is to multiply these gifts you've been given. To keep multiplying them even more or to start multiplying them even better. And you can do it. You *need* to do it. But one of the greatest secrets to doing it well comes from relying more heavily than ever on the opportunities found in community.

Let's say you're the first person, already serving well and consistently. Way to go. I love that. But the brightness of your future service will always be tied to how deeply you stay grounded in community. The enemy will always be on the lookout to poison your output and corrupt your motivations.

He wants you succumbing to the pull of pride. He wants you drawing inward from the fatigue of self-sacrifice. But as long as your perspectives on ministry are staying sharpened through ongoing accountability with others, your years of faithful service will only have begun to multiply.

Here's your hope, my friend: community will help you keep going great.

Or maybe you're that second type of person who's often driven to outdo others, who feels competitive in comparison to their talents, unconvinced that your (seemingly) less significant contributions are really making a difference. But by staying fully engaged in community, you'll discover that the needs in the body of Christ are always greater than any small group of people can reach on their own, and that the opportunities for caring and giving are larger than any single stream of ministry.

Here's your hope, my friend: community gives you room to do what *you* do.

Or, finally, maybe you'd admit you've basically been burying whatever talent God has given you. But when you make the decision to dive more fully into community, you won't be able to maintain that position of frightened inactivity for long. In caring for others, even in being cared for *by* others, the artificial restraints that you've bracketed around yourself will start to fall away, and you'll be actively looking for new ways to invest in these people that you're growing to love so much in Christ.

Caring community is your ticket out of fear and insecurity.

In one regard, this developing sense of community will help you *do* your part more capably and readily than you've done it in days past. But because you're opening your heart more authentically toward others, because you're letting others be a source of help to you rather than a threat or a bother, the care that you're both giving and receiving within community ensures you're *becoming* someone who looks more like Christ, not just performing or going through the motions.

So find your people and hold on to them. This doesn't mean you need to have eighty BFFs all giving you input on your schedule, your heart, your attitude, or your faithfulness. But find a few of them that you can commit to walking through life with, linking arms and sometimes holding each others' arms up when they're too weak to carry on.

Believe me, if you sat down with a friend and tried to discover what was keeping you from becoming your best self, you could come up with a thousand other ways to measure it than we did. I'm not acting like our focus on soul care and community care is the only way to look at it. But if you feel like you've lost yourself in the mad pursuit of what you're doing, maybe these two principles will help you get back on the right track.

Caring for your soul and inviting community into your life will not only benefit you in the short term, but you'll find them helping you persevere to the end of life still loving and following God. Instead of viewing them as something that will slow you down, view them through the lens of how Jesus viewed them. He valued caring for His soul. He valued caring for and being cared for by the people around Him. They didn't slow down His mission; they *were* His mission.

———

Sometimes work becomes my goal, not God.

Has that ever been true of you?

There have been times in my life—as a Christian author, as a Christian podcaster, as a Christian speaker and teacher and communicator—when I've almost shaken my head in disbelief because I haven't opened my Bible in a week. Shocking but true. This for sure happened when I had little kids at home who needed me for so many hours in the day. But can I just say, it's also happened since my kids have gotten big enough to be fully capable of pulling their own breakfast from the pantry and getting themselves completely ready every day.

The point I'm trying to make here is that we have a tendency to go too fast, thinking that our house, our job, our career, our educational pursuit or whatever will simply not happen if we ever give ourselves permission to slow down for a second. There's an unspoken mantra with women today that says we need to work extra hard to get the things we want. There are more memes about *working hard* out there than I can even count.

And while I like what I do (as I hope you do), and I think it's good for us to like what we do, I have a feeling we'll look backward someday from the distance of years at all we've done and we'll ask ourselves, "But who did I become?" And if I can't answer that question very well, not much of what I did is going to matter that much to me.

To quote Spurgeon again, "I wish not so much to do as to be, and I long to be like Jesus." I long to *become* like Jesus. Which means I don't need to be constantly chasing what I think I need to get done. I especially don't need to keep chasing what *others* are doing and how they get it done. If I want to become the person God made me to be in this life, I just need to be following Jesus.

Because here's the truth: We become who we follow. We become who is teaching us. We become who we spend time with. We become who we listen to.

This is no surprise to anyone who has children. We spend hours upon hours with our kids, and the things that usually frustrate us the most about them are the things they do that look JUST LIKE THE THINGS WE DO! Usually it's the very things that frustrate us the most about ourselves. Our kids mimic us because they're watching us and listening to us so closely.

Obviously there's nothing wrong with listening and learning from others in your field when they talk about how they achieved their success. I look up to many women who've carved the way, proving themselves faithful to where God has put them. But working hard to become *like* them should not be my ultimate goal. I can't want their success to be my success, or else I'll feel driven by misplaced motivations for why I do what I do.

My main focus can't be on *my* doing or *their* doing but on how well I'm following Jesus.

———

An Old Testament king named Ahaz was one of a long line of kings who sat on David's throne but "did not do what was right in the eyes of the LORD." What's worse, in the later days of his life, when he couldn't seem to deal with the pressure of enemy nations bearing down and threatening to destroy him, the Bible says he resorted to making sacrifices to foreign idols in a desperate attempt for something good to happen to him. "Because the gods of the kings of Syria helped them," he said, "I will sacrifice to them that they may help me." He looked around and saw what seemed to be working for others, and he assumed the same strategies would lead to his own success as well.

But we need only *one* God to follow, the way Mary (the sister of Lazarus) sought to listen and learn from Jesus. Maybe you remember the story where Jesus came to their home one day, and Mary's sister Martha immediately got up and started working around the house to be sure everything was perfect for Him, while Mary simply sat at His feet and listened to Him teach. Martha got so upset with her sister, even complaining to Jesus about it, asking Him to tell her to get in here and start helping out. "Martha, Martha," He patiently said, "you are anxious and troubled about many things, but one thing is necessary. Mary has chosen the good portion, which will not be taken away from her."

My ultimate goal in life, just as I hope it's your ultimate goal in life, is to become more like Christ in everything I do. I want to look more like Jesus as a mom, as a wife, as a friend, as a podcaster, as an author, as a neighbor, as a woman.

And if in all my doing, I look in the mirror like my friend did one day and "don't like who I'm becoming," I hope I'll do something to change it. I hope I'll follow Him out of my addiction to doing and discover what my life with Him is supposed to be about. And I have a sneaking suspicion you want the same thing too.

Chapter 10

Faithful to the End

Late July, 8:00 in the morning. I awoke to my phone buzzing.

It was summer, and that means Momma doesn't get up until Momma gets up! So I was aware of the buzzing, but I was also aware I had nothing on my calendar for the day, and whoever "needed" me could just wait while I squirreled away a few more minutes of sleep.

But the buzzes kept coming until I finally snatched up my phone to see what in the world was so important to somebody this early in the morning. Because in the summer, 8:00 is most definitely early to me.

The first thing I noticed was a number of Voxer messages from a group I'm in. Weird, though, because most of the messages referred to a specific person by name who wasn't even part of that group. Why would everybody be talking about *her*? I then kept seeing sad-face emojis and lots of OMGs, which were making my brain work really hard to try figuring out what was going on. The next thing I knew, I spotted a missed call from my friend Chrystal, just as a text popped up from her as well, saying, "Call me as soon as you can. It's about Wynter."

Uh-oh.

Even in my sleepy haze, the puzzle pieces started coming together: Wynter. Sad faces. OMG. A missed phone call from her cousin.

This didn't sound good.

I crept quietly downstairs, not wanting to wake any of my kids, and slipped out on the front porch. Sitting down, I placed the call to Chrystal. "Jamie," she said in a shaken, somber voice, "Wynter died last night."

What?! I sank deeper in my chair. That's impossible! How could Wynter be dead? She was so young, just thirty-eight. I'd texted her only recently when she'd told me she was planning a visit to Austin and was hoping we could get together. I hadn't been able to make things work that week, and in the shock of this sudden news, I was thinking how badly I wished I'd cleared my calendar for her. If I'd only known it would've been my last opportunity.

I didn't know what to say. But in the middle of my confused silence, Chrystal began piecing the details together for me, how Wynter had experienced unexpected heart failure at home in the late afternoon and had peacefully passed away—none of which made sense to me.

It didn't seem fair or right. How in the world did God see fit to take home this woman in the prime of her life? Married for fifteen years. Right in the middle of raising four beautiful daughters. Writing books left and right to encourage mommas and young girls. I felt certain we needed her here with us on Earth a lot more than He needed her there with Him right now. On the evening after her death, as members from her family gathered to talk about our hope amid this tragedy,[24] we couldn't help asking the questions we all find ourselves asking during times like that.

Why her?

Why now?

How is this good?

Losing someone to death that you loved so much in life—especially someone who seemed much too young to die—causes you to evaluate things. You look back on your encounters with them. You hope and pray they knew how much you loved them. You remember the moments you shared that were so monumental and special.

Wynter and I, for instance, had journeyed to Uganda together a few years earlier, and we'd stayed friends ever since.

---

[24] You can be part of that gathering yourself. Watch at https://www. youtube.com/watch?v=Y9JBd0xqBGQ.

She'd joined me on my podcast a few times and was set to be a guest at an event of mine in the fall. She was beautiful, brilliant, hilarious, and downright comfortable in who she was. I always admired the ease with which she went through life. She always seemed so secure and confident, knowing she was where she was supposed to be, both in her life and in her ministry.

Wynter's funeral was by far one of the best I've ever attended. It seems weird to qualify funerals as being good or bad, but I don't think I'm the only one who does that. You kind of know when it's good and you know when it's bad. Like, I'll bet you've attended a funeral or two in your time, as I have, that left you feeling sort of gross and yucky. Wynter's was so far from that. Her memorial service was completely uplifting, it glorified God, and it showcased one woman's faithfulness to Him in every way, in everything He'd given her.

I was so glad for the chance, around six months later, to express these things to her husband, Jonathan, while he was sharing his memories of Wynter with my listeners, talking about her testimony and legacy and the godly example she lived each day. When we got around to talking about her funeral, I was able to tell him what struck me the most from the whole service—how I didn't leave feeling sad (though of course I was sad), but instead left feeling hopeful and challenged. Encouraged and inspired.

Wynter, at thirty-eight, had been alive on Earth for around fourteen thousand days. And when I sum up her life, here's the phrase that comes to mind: *she used her days well.* Everyone who knew her would give you the same impression. It's the same story I hear from Jonathan, from her girls, from her cousins. It's what all of us say when we talk about Wynter.

And it's the same thought that has stuck with me ever since her passing. I pray it never leaves me. *I want to use my days well.* When I go to be with Jesus, I want people to be able to say of me, "Jamie was alive for (whatever number of) days, and she used each one of them well."

May the same be true for all of us.

That's how my friend Wynter lived, I can tell you that. She lived a life that mattered because she lived the life God had given her, utilizing the talents God had given her,[25] speaking with the voice God had given her, making the most of the passions and desires God had given her. Better yet, she put them all into action *right where she was,* not waiting for an opportunity to magically open up where she could finally turn them loose.

And if you ask me, that's how you and I, like Wynter, can be sure we come to the end of our days as the living pictures of success.

---

[25] Her magazine, *For Girls Like You,* still lives on. Check it out: https://forgirlslikeyou.com/.

———

Do you ever have any of those moments where you're minding your own business, just listening to a song, when all of a sudden your emotions begin to go crazy on you, and the next thing you know, you're crying? Not a few tears either. *Big* tears. And they won't stop. You really didn't see this coming.

That was me the other day while out on a walk with my dogs.

Walking the dogs in my neighborhood is a favorite pastime of mine. I almost always put in my headphones and escape into what's usually a fairly eclectic musical place. On this particular day I set my phone to start shuffling songs and just let it do its thing. I started out jamming to a Chris Stapleton song, followed by a cut from the soundtrack to *Hamilton*, and finally a song from Sara Groves, circa 2001, for sure an oldie but goodie! That was the random selection that worked me up into such an ugly cry that day. Sara Groves started singing, my heart began listening, my mouth started singing along, and the next thing I knew, I was sobbing.

Printed-out song lyrics rarely create the same effect, so I won't type them up for you here. But if you ever take my recommendation and go out there hunting for the song "This Journey Is My Own" from her 2001 album *Conversations*, I think you'll see why it gets me every time.

It *really* got me that day.

Because she's right. I really will reach the end of my time on the earth at some point, and I'll stand alone before the Lord with no one else accountable for what I did with my life. Except for me. And when I see with my own eyes the glory and power of the One who made me—the One who made me for Himself—and who for some completely unexplainable reason decided to forgive me and redeem me, I think I'll wonder why I ever cared for two seconds whether I got anybody else's approval for anything I did. Why did I yearn to hear my kids, my spouse, my peers, my parents tell me they accepted me or love me? His love and acceptance of me will be the only thing that matters in that moment.

And that's because His love for me is the only thing that matters in *this* moment, or in any one of our *right now* moments. For like Jesus said, "What does it profit a man to gain the whole world and forfeit his soul?" Living for the approval of other people only benefits us for the relatively few years that we spend here on Earth. All our striving to look the part does nothing for us. All my concern about whether or not I was impressing people with my talents, my ideas, my personality, my insights, my parenting, my marriage, or anything else will prove to have been just a complete waste of time and emotional energy.

But to live and breathe for that "audience of One" (as Sara Groves says in her song), the way we'll shout and praise Him in that moment, standing there (kneeling there, falling facedown in front of Him there), existing for the first time in His visible presence, will be like the greatest sense of relief we've ever experienced.

And—excuse me while I wipe away the tears that are leaking from the corners of my eyes again right now—I'm just done carrying around the weight that comes from doing anything else. I'm done with being upset if my life doesn't seem to be measuring up to how other people are doing theirs. I'm living the rest of my life for Him—for *Him*!

This journey is my own.

And my journey belongs to Jesus.

This right-here, right-now journey that He's put me on . . .

I'm living the rest of it in faithfulness to Him and Him alone.

And why don't you just come along and join me, in the right-there, right-this-moment places of opportunity and influence where He's created you to serve Him with your own calling, voice, and passions?

I believe I could do without the pressure of doing anything else.

And I believe we'll get His "well done" if we do.

————

I get it though—those times when you just really have a hard time feeling satisfied with your right-here, right-now life. I think a lot of us feel that way on a lot of days. But as you and I get close to the end of our time together in this book, I want to give you another reason why we ought to throw that feeling out the front door whenever it sneaks in the back.

Jesus said, referring to all of us, "You are the light of the world," like a "city set on a hill," like a lamp burning on a lampstand that "gives light to all in the house."

Let that sink in for just a bit.

I think we'd all agree our world is a pretty dark place. I have a hard time watching the news anymore or logging on to Twitter and reading what people are talking about and commenting on, because of how dark everything seems. It's all around us. Just *darkness*.

But because of Jesus in us, we are "the light of the world." Amazing. Actually He Himself is "the light of the world," He said, so that "whoever follows me will not walk in darkness but will have the light of life." That's how even such fallen, darkened people as ourselves become able to be a light for others to notice. His light, the light of Jesus, burns from within us.

It's what we're here to do.

A couple of years ago we hosted a gathering at our home for a fundraiser. It was a beautiful event that raised a lot of money to be put toward some God-honoring work. But one of the best things that happened that night occurred after the event was already over, during the cleanup.

The restaurant that catered it sent out some of their best workers, and Aaron and I truly enjoyed getting to know them, talk with them, and enjoy their time in our home. After most of the hard work was done, Aaron was hanging out with a few of them in his recording studio, and one of them said, "You know, there's something different about you guys. We've catered a lot of events, but we rarely get welcomed and treated like this. Y'all are just so nice."

I was sure grateful to hear that. I mean, I like to think we come off as nice people. But I believe what they were really responding to was the "light" they hopefully saw and felt from us. There ought to be something different, something noticeable about people who carry the light of Jesus inside, into all of their everyday moments. We ought to draw others out of the darkness that pinches in so hard and heavy on them all the time and make them want to be near the light.

But that's not really the main reason for this light—you know, having people think we're nice and all. The reason it's so valuable (and so exciting!) for us to simply shine in whatever places God has put us is because of what Jesus said this "light" of ours is actually able to accomplish. "Let your light shine before others," He said, "so that they may see your good works and give glory to your Father who is in heaven."

Okay, wait a minute, I'm about to get fired up again. He's saying that when we just do what we believers in Jesus are each equipped to do—shine with the light of Christ inside us—He gets glory from that? My audience of One feels glorified? The only One whose approval of me ever really matters says, *I love how you show Me off when you do that?*

Then I just want to stop and ask myself, What's not to love about *that*? Why should I worry about whether my light is as bright as anyone else's if Jesus has already said He gets glory from the amount of light that's shining through me right here, right now?

What else do I want? What else do I need? As long as God is getting the glory He deserves.

———

Way back in the Old Testament, God was already telling His people that their job was not to be impressive—at least not to be impressive on the basis of their own ability, presentation, or performance. "It was not because you were more in number than any other people that the LORD set his love on you and chose you," He told them, "for you were the fewest of all peoples." He wasn't depending on them to make a big splash or to wow everybody with their obvious gifts and abilities.

Here's what set them apart instead. Here's *all* that set them apart and made them special. "It is because the LORD loves you and is keeping the oath that he swore to your fathers, that the LORD has brought you out with a mighty hand and redeemed you from the house of slavery, from the hand of Pharaoh king of Egypt."

You remember that story, I'll bet—how the Israelite people were held as slaves in Egypt for roughly four centuries, bound to cruel taskmasters until God set them free and relocated them in the Promised Land.

But you know what? That's not just an old, old, Old Testament story. It's the story that God is still writing through your life right here today.

Over in 1 Peter, the old apostle who'd once denied *three times* in *one night* that he was a follower of Jesus said that we as believers in Christ are "a chosen race, a royal priesthood, a holy nation, a people for his own possession." Again, it's not because we're so impressive in our own right. In fact, "once you were not a people, but now you are God's people; once you had not received mercy, but now you have received mercy."

And because our God has been willing to do this amazing thing for us—redeem us from all our guilt, shame, and punishment and everything else that ought to come along with our miserably sinful condition—He gives us the opportunity every day of our lives to "proclaim the excellencies of him who called you out of darkness into his marvelous light."

Pretty cool, huh?

So tell me: Why does this calling and assignment He's given us—the one He's given to you, given to me, given to each of us in our own unique settings and situations—why is it any less valuable or important than the calling and assignment He's given to anyone else?

You don't just shine with a generic, feel-good light. You shine with a glorious gospel light, a light that shows everyone in your field of vision what Jesus can do with any person who puts their trust in Him.

It's been like that forever. I've seen it with my own eyes.

I think of my grandparents, who walked faithfully with the Lord until their last breath on this earth. They weren't well known. Neither of them had a huge platform or anything. But their faithfulness to their callings, their faithful use of their voices and influence sure did impact *my* life in a remarkable way.

I'm so thankful my grandmother got to hear me share my testimony of God's saving grace in my life at a women's event she was able to attend. I'm glad she was there at the first *Happy Hour Live!* event held at my house, where I was able to lift high the name of Jesus in such a public way. I'm glad she was there to see it because she died only three months later, but I am still telling others what her faithfulness helped create in my life.

She was always serving at her church in some way, whether through the pregnancy center, the library, or the kids' programs. Most of the time when she arrived at church, she had one of her great-grandchildren in tow. She wasn't babysitting them, though their parents no doubt enjoyed the small break she provided them. She was including those little ones in what she was doing, all with the hope that they too would follow Jesus one day. She knew there was more to life than retiring and laying low until her time here was over. She never wavered in wanting to influence the people around her.

My grandfather had no less of an impact, both on myself and others, in his own unique way. In 2006, Marie Parker authored a book about my grandfather titled *Major Choctaw*. He'd already passed away by that time, but as I devoured every word, I realized how much my grandfather had overcome in his life. He was orphaned at eight years old by his mother who was fleeing an abusive relationship. He grew up in an Indian orphanage, where he endured discrimination, racial slurs, and abuse because of his heritage. Alcoholism, depression, war, famine, and poverty all encompassed his life, but at some point he decided to follow Jesus. His life was forever changed. And the grandfather I knew for twenty-four years of my life constantly pointed me toward Jesus.

Their impact extended far beyond their earthly years, just as yours and mine will do as well—not because our lives are the essence of worldly success, but simply because we have the chance each day to be faithful.

These journeys of ours are the only ones we'll get to take, these journeys we're making before the Lord. And whether they seem to matter or not to us, in the pitiful way we so often judge such things, they matter to those who will come behind us. Your impact, your legacy—it matters. What we do with our time on the earth matters for the faith of those coming behind us.

Just like I remember my grandparents who came before me, I'm certain you can name someone (perhaps many someones) who outrageously, incalculably impacted your faith.

The power of their words and example proclaimed to you the wonder of a God who called them "out of darkness into his marvelous light." And because they were faithful with that mission, most likely over many years, you stand here today as someone who lives in that light as well.

And the sooner you grow comfortably content with the opportunities God has given you to do the same thing for others, the more chances you'll find to be that same kind of influence in your right-here, right-now sphere of connection.

I recently attended two baptisms. One was in the waters of the Gulf of Mexico while we were at our church's youth camp in Panama City, Florida; the other was in the swimming pool in a couple's backyard here in Texas.

At the one in Florida, my husband and I baptized two of our own kids, which made it an unforgettable time of celebration in our family. There's not much better in life than seeing your kids develop their own love for Jesus. Watching them declare that they were dedicating their life to the Lord in front of their friends is something I'll never forget.

But I want to close this book with a quick story about the other ceremony I attended, and about the other two people Aaron baptized.

They were husband and wife. We met them not long after moving to Austin. On their patio in the backyard before the baptism ceremony, we stood around with them and their five children, as well as a few other couples who'd befriended them through the years. One of the couples, with whom they'd been longtime neighbors, recounted the many times they'd prayed for God to reveal Himself to these dear friends so that they could know and experience His great love for them in Christ. Others shared their own thoughts and words of encouragement before we clasped hands and sang songs together declaring the goodness of God.

His goodness toward them. His goodness toward us.

During one of the songs we sang, I noticed the wife smiling even more broadly than before, getting emotional as she laid her head back, closed her eyes, and praised her newfound Savior. After we finished and the praises died down a bit, she told us how that song brought back such vivid memories of her grandparents, who took her to church as a little girl, who told her about Jesus, and many times prayed over her life, that she would come to know the Lord. "How Great Thou Art," she recalled hearing them sing in church. It was as though, on her backyard patio, she could almost hear their voices singing that song on either side of her.

Wow, and now I'm crying again, just thinking of it.

Her grandparents weren't there in person to see the fruit of the prayers they'd prayed over their beloved little granddaughter. But can you imagine the day they reunite with her in God's presence, in the new heaven and earth? Their influence, their actions, their faithfulness just to "be themselves" for this one special person in their lives had come full circle. It was not in vain. Their lives were so much bigger than the seemingly small footprint they made. It was big enough and used by God enough to track down a forty-five-year-old woman with the grace that flowed from a wooden, bloody cross. And in their pool that day, surrounded by their kids, we were able to celebrate the fact that Jesus' amazing mercy had washed all this granddaughter's sins away.

Your life matters. Every minute of it matters.

But will there be generations to look back and know they've been changed because of the influence we faithfully exercised during our time here? Will there be children, grandchildren, friends, even total strangers, who can say of us, like we all said of Wynter at her funeral, that we lived our days well? That we lived them in faithfulness to our callings?

That we lived them for Jesus alone?

Hebrews 12 begins with a "therefore." This means the amazing accounts of Hebrews 11, where the writer of that book recounted the life stories of people like Abraham, Sarah, Moses, and others, actually has a direct tie-in to the journeys that you and I are living today. Because of the lives they lived, the author has something to say to us about how we should live.

> Therefore, since we are surrounded by so
> great a cloud of witnesses, let us also lay aside
> every weight, and sin which clings so closely,

and let us run with endurance the race that
is set before us, looking to Jesus, the founder
and perfecter of our faith, who for the joy
that was set before him endured the cross,
despising the shame, and is seated at the right
hand of the throne of God.

This is our challenge: to run with endurance the race that
is set before us. He has a plan for your life. A *great* plan. A *big*
plan. And He has given you everything you need to help you
run your race well. He's given you the example of His only
Son and the enabling of His Holy Spirit. There is no reason
to try convincing everyone how awesome you are or how
much better you can do it. We're not running on competitive
tracks. We're only running to hear the applause of our Lord
and King telling us we shone His light and brought Him
glory.

So my prayer for you as you continue your journey
through this lifetime is that you would throw off anything—
anything!—that is holding you down, and that you would
live freely as a woman who trusts in her Maker and believes
He can do priceless things through your life. Run confidently
down these paths He has set for you, and show everyone in
sight what your God has done, what your God can do.

Show them He's doing it right here, right now. In you.

ACKNOWLEDGMENTS

Nothing good happens alone. It's true. I'm grateful for all of the people who surround me, help me, build me up, cheer me on, correct my mistakes, and help me get messages like this one out to the world. This book was loved on by so many humans, and here are some of them I would like to thank.

My entire team at B&H. You guys have been the absolute best to work with. I'm honored to run this race with you all. Devin, Ashley, Mary, Jenaye, Lawrence, and everyone else who worked on this project. Huge thanks to you all! You have cared for this project well, and I'm so grateful for that.

Jenni Burke, you are a joy to have in my corner. There's nothing, I know, you won't help me with! Annie, Anna, Staci, Becca, and Sally—that roundtable meeting meant more to me than you will ever know.

Amanda and Aki, I love working with you both. Lyndsey, the glue you provide to all I have going on in my life is so valuable to me!

Amy, Leslie, Lindsey, Noelle, Catherine, Taylor, and Angela, thank you for praying for this project.

Lysa, that day in your home spurred me on more than you will ever know. Thank you all for loving me, believing in me, praying for me, and helping me in my journey of faithfulness.

To the listeners of *The Happy Hour with Jamie Ivey*, you are truly the best, and I'm so thankful that every week you trust me enough to put my show in your earbuds as you walk, wash dishes, drive to work, grocery shop, or whatever you might be doing on a Wednesday morning!

Aaron, your belief in me and my work is greater than I deserve. Thanks for loving me well and pushing me to do more than I ever thought I could.

Cayden, Amos, Deacon, and Story, you are my greatest accomplishments, and I pray that one day when you decide it's cool to read the books your mom wrote, you will treasure these words. I believe so deeply that you have a great purpose in this world and your faithfulness is all God wants from you!

God, this is all for you. Take these words and do something with them.

SCRIPTURE VERSE REFERENCES

(by page number)

Chapter 1: Good Time for a You-Turn?

6: "already numbered, planned, and written for you" (Ps. 139:16; Job 14:5)

7: "only good things coming from you and me are coming from the Father" (James 1:17)

Chapter 2: Faithfulness Comes First

23: "Go therefore and make disciples" (Matt. 28:19–20)

25: "You are the light of the world" (Matt. 5:14–16)

29: "Shall a child be born" (Gen. 17:17)

29: "He said, 'Take your son'" (Gen. 22:2–3)

36: "light" (Ps. 119:105)

36: "living and active" (Heb. 4:12)

36: "breathed out" (2 Tim. 3:16)

36: "Do not be conformed" (Rom. 12:2)

37: "I will ask the Father" (John 14:16–17)

Chapter 6: Selfie Satisfaction

124: "Now the serpent was more crafty" (Gen. 3:1)

124: "You may surely eat of every tree" (Gen. 2:16–17)

125: "We may eat of the fruit of the trees" (Gen. 3:2–3)

126: "The serpent said to the woman" (Gen. 3:4–5)

126: "So when the woman saw" (Gen. 3:6)

127: "the eyes of both were opened" (Gen. 3:7)

130: "I do not understand my own actions" (Rom. 7:15)

131: "I can do all things through him" (Phil. 4:13)

132: "For I have learned" (Phil. 4:11)

133: "I know how to be brought low" (Phil. 4:12)

135: "all things that pertain to life" (2 Pet. 1:3)

135: "By this my Father is glorified" (John 15:8)

136: "love, joy, peace" (Gal. 5:22–23)

136: "Abide in me, and I in you" (John 15:4)

137: "I am the vine" (John 15:5)

Chapter 7: Unavoidable but Invaluable

150: "cannot serve God and money" (Matt. 6:24)

151: "rejoice" (Rom. 5:3)

151: "Count it all joy" (James 1:2–4)

154: "rejoice in our sufferings" (Rom. 5:3–5)

157: "Everyone who hears these words of mine" (Matt. 7:26–27)

158: "Everyone then who hears" (Matt. 7:24–25)

EXCERPT REFERENCES

(by page number)

Chapter 2: Faithfulness Comes First

25: "Talents and burdens collide"
Rebekah Lyons, *You Are Free* (Grand Rapids, MI: Zondervan, 2017), 51.

32: "Dethroning the idols of Christian marriage"
Kat Armstrong, *No More Holding Back* (Nashville: W Publishing, 2019), 42.

Chapter 5: Going Green

98: "Insecurity is both the root of comparison"
Richella J. Parham, *Mythical Me* (Downers Grove, IL: IVP, 2019), 21.

98: "Whatever aspect of ourselves we might be measuring"
Ibid.

104: "Comparison has a pull to it"
Lisa Bevere, *Without Rival* (Grand Rapids, MI: Revell, 2016), 86.

111: "You can't obey God in someone else's life"
"Comparison," interview with Abigail Dodds, *Journeywomen* podcast, episode 94, August 12, 2019, https://journeywomen podcast.com/episode/comparison.

113: "The more beauty we find in someone else's journey"
Bob Goff, https://twitter.com/bobgoff/status/10065375346 44469760?lang=en.

Chapter 6: Selfie Satisfaction

133: "a point of contentment"
Larry Fitzmaurice, "*Lover* is pure Taylor Swift, at her most content and confident," August 23, 2019, https://ew.com/music /2019/08/23/taylor-swift-lover-review/.

134: "Contentment is not finally getting to a place"
Patricia Miller and Rachel Gorman, *God's Wisdom for Women* (Grand Rapids, MI: Baker, 2017), 43.

137: "Greek word for 'abide' is *meno*"
James Strong, *A Concise Dictionary of the Words in the Greek Testament*, 47; Biblestudytools.com.

Chapter 7: Unavoidable but Invaluable

145: "If we really want to start down the road"
Michael Kelley, *Wednesdays Were Pretty Normal* (Nashville: B&H, 2012), 44.

146: "God made it matter"
The Happy Hour with Jamie Ivey, episode 278, January 1, 2020; https://jamieivey.com/278-beth-moore.

146: "It's a journey of trying to embrace the fact"
Michael Kelley, *Wednesdays Were Pretty Normal* (Nashville: B&H, 2012), 17.

148: "Retha Nichole"
The Happy Hour with Jamie Ivey, episode 77, February 26, 2016, https://jamieivey.com/happy-hour-77-retha-nichole/.

148: "Kate Merrick"
The Happy Hour with Jamie Ivey, episode 133, March 22, 2017, https://jamieivey.com/the-happy-hour-133-kate-merrick/ ALSO: episode 243, May 1, 2019, https://jamieivey.com/243-kate -merrick/.

148: "I've learned not to fear suffering"
Kate Merrick, *And Still She Laughs* (Nashville: Nelson, 2017), 11.

148: "Rachel Henry"
The Happy Hour with Jamie Ivey, episode 196, June 6, 2018, https://jamieivey.com/the-happy-hour-196-rachel-henry/.

148: "Lauren Scruggs Kennedy"
The Happy Hour with Jamie Ivey, episode 137, April 19, 2017, https://jamieivey.com/happy-hour-137-lauren-scruggs-kennedy/.

152: "Katherine Wolf"
The Happy Hour with Jamie Ivey, episode 98, July 21, 2016, https://jamieivey.com/happy-hour-98-katherine-wolf/.

156: "God is not in the business"
Courtney Reissig, "You Can't Turn Lemons into Lemonade," December 2, 2013, https://www.thegospelcoalition.org/article /you-cant-turn-lemons-into-lemonade/.

159: "In this life, we will have trouble"
Lore Ferguson Wilbert, "In This Life You Will Grow Up," October 15, 2018, https:// lifewayvoices.com/culture-current -events/in-this-life-you-will-grow-up/.

160: "If we knew what God knows"
Tim Keller, https://twitter.com/timkellernyc/status/4253100 26203680768.

Chapter 8: Bloom Where You're Planted

171: "Annie Downs's *That Sounds Fun* podcast"
http://www.anniefdowns.com/2019/09/06/episode-165 -jenn-jett-camp-well/.

180: "God has made you what you are"
Charles Spurgeon, *Spurgeon's Sermons Volume 18:1872*, 256.

Chapter 9: Between Doing and Being

186: "I wish not so much to do as to be"
The Valley of Vision: A Collection of Puritan Prayers & Devotions, edited by Arthur Bennett, Banner of Truth Trust, 1975, 127.

198: "I wish not so much to do as to be"
Ibid.

Chapter 10: Faithful to the End

204: "Jonathan Pitts"
The Happy Hour with Jamie Ivey, episode 232, February 13, 2019, https://jamieivey.com/232-jonathan-pitts/.

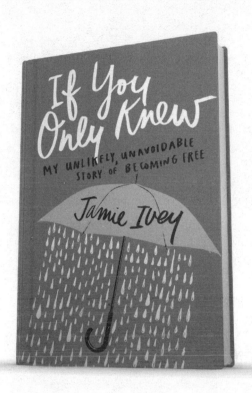

the *happy hour*
with Jamie Ivey

THE HAPPY HOUR IS A PLACE WHERE FRIENDS GATHER TO TALK ABOUT THE BIG THINGS IN LIFE, THE LITTLE THINGS IN LIFE, AND EVERYTHING IN BETWEEN. EACH WEEK ON THE PODCAST, JAMIE AND A GUEST INVITE YOU INTO THEIR CONVERSATION, AND YOU WILL BE INSPIRED, ENCOURAGED, AND POINTED TO JESUS THROUGH EVERY SHOW.

LISTEN HERE:

APPLE PODCAST

SPOTIFY

OVERCAST

CONNECT WITH JAMIE:

WWW.JAMIEIVEY.COM
@JAMIEIVEY